TO ENTERTAIN

TO ENTERTAIN
INSTRUCTIONS FOR A DINNER PARTY

JAGO RACKHAM

ROBINSON

ROBINSON

First published in Great Britain in 2026 by Robinson

3 5 7 9 10 8 6 4 2

Copyright © Jago Rackham, 2026
Illustrations by Faye Wei Wei

The moral right of the author has been asserted.

All rights reserved.
No part of this publication may be reproduced, stored in a retrieval system, or transmitted, in any form, or by any means, without the prior permission in writing of the publisher, nor be otherwise circulated in any form of binding or cover other than that in which it is published and without a similar condition including this condition being imposed on the subsequent purchaser.

A CIP catalogue record for this book
is available from the British Library.

ISBN: 978-1-40878-328-3

Designed by Clare Sivell
Typeset in Adobe Garamond Pro by Clare Sivell
Printed and bound in Great Britain by Clays Ltd, Elcograf S.p.A.

Papers used by Robinson are from well-managed forests
and other responsible sources.

Robinson
An imprint of
Little, Brown Book Group
Carmelite House
50 Victoria Embankment
London EC4Y 0D

The authorised representative
in the EEA is
Hachette Ireland
8 Castlecourt Centre, Dublin 15,
D15 XTP3, Ireland
(email: info@hbgi.ie)

An Hachette UK Company
www.hachette.co.uk

www.littlebrown.co.uk

To Ló

Contents

Acknowledgements	ix
Introduction: Granny's Account Book	x
DINNERS	1
GUESTS	57
GUESTING	67
THE ROOM AND THE TABLE	79
WHAT TO MAKE	101
DINNER ITSELF	119
RECIPES	161
Index	237

Acknowledgements

With thanks to Tosia Leniarska whose intellectual and emotional generosity was integral to this book's creation, to Felix and Sally for looking over the manuscript, to Ben for his initial push, and to my agent Daisy for her constant support.

While writing, I play songs on repeat, and their rhythms are integral to the book's metre. Most important is Handel's Organ Concerto in G Minor, Op 7, No.5, HWV: II *Adante larghetto e staccato*, which – in various recordings – has defined my writing life. I madly finished my rough copy for Lutyens and Rubinstein while listening to 'Electricity' by Orchestral Manoeuvres in the Dark, finished my first draft while listening to 'Broccoli' by DRAM feat. Lil Yachty, and responded to edits while listening to 100 Gecs' 'Hollywood Baby'.

Granny's Account Book

It begins with a fable, sort of. I was sitting in my aunt's house, with her and my father, going through papers she'd hung on to. Every family has an archivist. Here, a letter from my father, nine years old, just after being sent to boarding school: 'I do miss everyone very much but I am learning the ropes.' What my aunt was looking for, what we had spent the afternoon discussing, was my granny's account book. In it she recorded everything she'd cooked for dinner parties, all the drinks she'd served, and what it all cost, to the penny, as well as every guest present. Granny had to entertain because she was an officer's wife. Weekly, twice a week; sometimes for my grandfather's superiors, sometimes for junior officers.

The account book served a dual purpose – to ensure she did not serve the same dish twice and to make sure she did not overspend. She and my grandfather were not, as many of the British officer class were, independently wealthy – she was the daughter of a single mother and had grown up as a poor cousin in an aunt's house, somewhere between guest and servant. Grandfather was the son of grocers and petty criminals from Portsmouth. And so, all this entertaining – and military tailoring, boarding school, keeping up the appearance of being much richer than they were – was done on a comparatively small salary. I like to think that for my grandparents, the British Army was not something of particular pride, but an escape from closet bedrooms and the price of cabbage.

I wish my grandfather had been a civil servant – anything but a soldier! I cannot wish my granny had been anything else, for the condition of a wife of her class would have been much the same no matter her husband's job, though with more constancy and a little more money. What her account book expresses is a woman doing as so many women do: making much out of little with apparent ease. Hosting – women's work – was both calling and profession, expressive of ingenuity and creativity.

That was years ago. We never found the account book, and it was only remembered when I decided to write this book. I'd been at my maternal grandma's, bothering her about the food she'd cooked in the English suburbs of the sixties and seventies. Going through her cookbooks she found her first, an instructional book for new wives from her mother. 'I can't imagine giving anything like this to *your* mother . . . ' The book was dirty in the way old cookbooks ought to be – beef stew from the seventies on the page for beef stew, now a shadowish mark. The writing was stilted and patronising. But the base instructional nature of the book spoke to me. How often had friends of mine said that they did not know how to have people to dinner, or that they were nervous to do so, or – most heartbreaking – that they were nervous to have me specifically? And so I thought I could impart some of my own scrimping and saving, my budgeting and note-taking, my attempts at sprezzatura and ritual, into such a book.

DINNERS

Dinners are not about the food, they are about the people at the table. This is a sentiment I will express again and again. But it is not *quite* so. For the food is not incidental, nor unimportant. Obviously. Food is what casts the spell and directs the guests. It can be formal, comforting or exciting. We eat elaborately when celebrating, to mark the occasion, and simply when we are seeing old friends. Context is everything, but context must be created. Host, you may play God. And like God, must know how far to extend yourself – a Tuesday may not offer the time a Sunday does. You must plan within your limits, and in so doing will flourish.

Weeknights

The big table was a touch damp under my hands, so must have been wiped just before we arrived. I wonder who does the table wiping here? V— is already sitting, while J— is clanging about with a large pot of almost-boiling water. 'There's wine in the jug', he says, over his shoulder, and V— springs up to get us glasses, but the doorbell rings and she disappears. Guests arrive, friendly, sweaty from the Tube, and then the evening is quickening like the boiling water. V— brings a large bowl of green salad and J— a saucepan of spaghetti with tomato sauce, which we eat with glasses and glasses of cheap red wine from the jug, often refilled.

When entertaining on a weeknight there are two things to consider: most of the time you'll have been working and will be working tomorrow too. So the effort you put in should reflect this, while the mood should not be so excessive that, if you care about such things, you end up staying up very late. Remember, you're stuck until the last guest is out the door. To allow enough time, tell guests to arrive around eight and plan to eat around nine, when everyone will have settled. Have snacks – pickles, crisps – on the table and make sure no one's hungry; most won't have eaten since lunch. Offer bread and butter, cheese and crackers, something quick and easy.

Do not worry about dressing yourself or your table too much, since you want to keep a weeknight dinner informal. Imagine you're in a grand house eating not in the dining room, with its chandeliers and silverware, but in the dim light of the kitchen. Your guests, tired from work, will appreciate this softened atmosphere.

Don't make cocktails (not strong ones anyway) on weeknights, since some guests can't help themselves. Instead, offer beer or wine, and in summer serve a spritz over ice made with two-thirds white wine and one-third soda water. Pleasing, cheap and unlikely to get anyone drunk before dinner. Keep the wine topped up throughout dinner but keep your own contribution to a bottle, if your guests have brought wine, and a maximum of two if there's the need. Try to keep consumption to four bottles between eight people, placing the wine your guests have brought somewhere away from the table after they give it to you. And if there is any left over at the end of the night, keep it for the next time you're entertaining – a small bounty.

You have a choice between making something simple and quick on the night – pasta, a salad, poached pears – or something more elaborate the night before – a stew, a soup, an infused cake. I cook on the night with old friends, those I'm comfortable with and don't need to attend to, since cooking while they're around adds to the pleasure. If

I'm having newer people over, I like to make as much of the meal as I can the night before, so that I'm not kept away from the conversation. After such preparation, cooking becomes a matter of turning your stew to a low heat, then making whatever you want to serve it with – blanched cabbage, polenta, simple peas. Another advantage of cooking beforehand is that any food that leans toward the liquid improves with a night's rest.

Serve coffee and tea with dessert and bring out your fruit bowl. After this, most guests will follow social conventions and leave, and those who don't can be herded out with yawns and pointed comments.

If, however, you want your Tuesday dinner to flow deep into Wednesday morning, treat it like Friday or Saturday.

Cavolo Nero and Farro Soup

A few years ago, we collected strays – three, four, five – who would eat often in our tiny kitchen. One day they appeared after Lo' and I had been in Florence, where I'd had a delicious farro soup that I was still thinking about, so I made this approximation.

SERVES 4

300g farro
1 large carrot, roughly chopped
3 sticks of celery, roughly chopped
1 white onion, peeled and roughly chopped
Olive oil
1 tsp fennel seeds
4 cloves of garlic, peeled and crushed
4 good quality pork sausages, chopped
1 x 400g tin of whole tomatoes, blitzed or mashed
A glug of red wine
A large bunch of cavolo nero, finely sliced
2 chicken stock pots
Sea salt and freshly ground black pepper

---

1. Place the farro in a pan of water – as much as if you were cooking pasta – and bring to a brisk boil. This will give time for the farro to be softened while you take care of everything else.
2. Add the carrot, celery and onion to a large pan and fry in a

generous glug of oil, along with the fennel seeds, until the onion begins to turn translucent.
3. Add the garlic and sausages and fry until the garlic is golden, stirring often, then add the tomatoes.
4. Reduce a little, then add a glug of red wine. Reduce once more, then mix in the cavolo nero.
5. Once the farro is cooked – which should take about 30 minutes or so; if not, cook for a little longer until tender – drain over a jug to catch the cooking water. Top up the liquid to 1.5 litres using hot water from the kettle. Reserving the cooking water saves the starch, which gives the soup a softer texture. Add the stock pots to the liquid in the jug and stir to dissolve.
6. Add the stock and the farro to the pan, bring to the boil, then simmer with the lid off for half an hour or so. Season to taste.

Roast's Ragu

A good cook avoids surplus and meanness and so walks a tightrope: food should never be wasted and no one should leave the table hungry. Missing either outcome should be the source of embarrassment, nay shame. It's lucky, then, that most food is just as good the next day and some is even better. This is a ragu for already-cooked lamb shoulder, but it works just as well with any other meat too fatty to be eaten as a cold cut. It is also changeable according to the hunger, greed or number of your guests – it may be meaty, or a tomato sauce graced by the richness of lamb and the hint of herbs.

SERVES 8

2 onions, peeled
1 carrot
1 stick of celery
2 cloves of garlic
Olive oil
Leftover lamb shoulder, roughly chopped
Glass of red wine
3 x 400g tins of whole tomatoes
Sea salt

---

1. Dice the onions, carrot, celery and garlic and fry in a pan with a glug of olive oil over a medium heat until the onion is golden.
2. Add the lamb; generally the fattier bits will be left, which is a good

thing. Fry until the fat begins to melt, then add the wine to deglaze the pan.
3. Blitz the tomatoes then add along with a generous pinch of salt. Bring to the boil, then reduce the heat and simmer gently, stirring every now and then, until the sauce is thick. Taste for seasoning and add pasta cooking water if it needs loosening up.

Friday and Saturday

Up the stairs and into a roomy and sunny studio, with a table in the middle – on it a plethora of tinned fish (sardines, razor clams, eels, smaller sardines?), a large slab of very good-looking foie gras, a plate of jamón, salad, lemons. S– shows me different seasonings she has – one is a Korean seaweed powder and another is a salt made by a perfumer in London, each of which she describes in her soft voice, an elongation of vowels rather than an accent. On various surfaces are other tasty things – bread on a pile of books, cheeses and strawberries atop the kiln, and before H–'s small pen sculptures are two polystyrene trays of oysters on shaved ice. White wine is opened; S– explains that it's grown on rocky soil in Austria, unusual for a riesling, near apricots, which she says you can taste. I take a small sip – it is savoury, clean. S– keeps saying everything is chaotic when it is actually exquisite, and says I should write about the flurry before guests arrive – I make notes on my phone.

I have never had a steady nine-to-five job, five days a week, and so have not had a practical reason to hold Friday and Saturday in high esteem. If I were a proper bohemian I wouldn't notice, but I'm still part of the world and find the weekend retains the same magic and permissiveness it had when I was at school. As on secular and religious holidays, there is pleasure in observing the same way almost everyone else does, even if their meanings are lost to you. And so, Monday to Friday I drag myself to my desk and keep the hours of a clerk and rest on Saturday and the Sabbath.

While their tempo is similar, Friday and Saturday dinners differ in prep time. If you're working, treat the food at your Friday dinner the way you would any other weekday. If you aren't working, or it's Saturday, let dinner become the day's purpose. I love to go to a market or the shops, buy what's good and let that decide what to cook. It is a joy, too, to spend the day in and out of the kitchen, doing laundry and putting up shelves, between slicing and stirring. Time makes dinner a creative endeavour.

Lo' begins making a cake and tells us to go shopping for roses and meat without her. After the flower market, we walk to Bethnal Green Road. It is thronged with Bangladeshis in their formal wear, coming from celebrating Boishakhi Mela in Weavers Fields after the procession through Banglatown. In the grocer's, I chat with D—, who is always here, and buy yellow and dark red tomatoes, goaty Serbian feta cheese, peaches, strawberries, bunches of mint and dill. Then to the halal butcher to buy

a lamb shoulder. I admire their posters: a cute lamb beneath a picture of a dolphin in a tropical sea. The butcher slices frozen fish into chunks; P– says this was the sound of their childhood in Nigeria, and Y– says that because she grew up in Trinidad she has little memory of frozen fish, only fish caught fresh and grilled quickly. Walking up the street I feel the sweetness of life in the summer: very free, my hands heavy with good food and lightened by good living. We buy cava – which the Americans call Champagne – beer and white wine.

At home we greet Lo' in the kitchen, still making cake. Outside are two guests; one, H–, is wearing black lipstick, looking like they'd gorged on blackcurrants. I bring out the meat, fruit and spices and we all chop peaches and strawberries, pressing them, with herbs and salt, into the lamb under the shade of the awning. I am impressed when H– goes straight in with their hands, rubbing peach into the meat, impressed by this friendly sort of confidence.

On nights I expect to be late I'll invite guests for eight thirty, which gives me time to get into the right mood for hosting – listen to music, dress, have a drink. If we serve food around nine thirty, it means eating will be done a little before eleven, opening up the rest of the night, allowing people to move from their chairs to different rooms, to embrace fluidity, to invite new people over or venture out.

Since you'll be eating late, it's good to have snacks on the table, though these should be measured against what you're serving. A roast duck and potatoes shouldn't follow tinned fish with thick slabs of bread and butter, and would welcome crisps, olives, pickled vegetables and the like. But bread and fish would be perfect before a brothy soup.

Make cocktails. Something a few people do, but I've never managed, is to make batch cocktails – this works with stirred cocktails, like Negronis, but not those that have soda water or are shaken, like a Martini. I like the showiness of making cocktails for my guests, so I'm happy to rise from the table to provide more. It's also a nice job to give someone else – in the fifties it was the role of the eldest child – but only if you trust them to. Whether or not you're making cocktails, make sure there's a bag of ice in the freezer. This often means asking someone to bring one, since the need always arises and a drink that becomes watery with one quick-melting ice cube is disgusting.

Otherwise, don't worry about how much is drunk; this should progress naturally. I usually have red or white wine available, or beer. The wine you serve first should be reasonably good, but a sensible host keeps a couple of cheap bottles aside to bring to the table when everything else has gone and your guests are too drunk to notice their quality. This will make you a hero and save expensive trips to the off-licence for expensive wine of mediocre quality. If more is wanted after your stash is depleted, let someone else go out.

If you wish to continue with the evening – after all, you needn't wake up tomorrow – bring strong coffee to the table, with a digestif – dessert wine, amaro, et cetera – a spirit, or more of what you've spent the evening drinking. Clear plates but not glasses, top up everyone's water, turn the music up a little. Of course, if you're flagging and don't want to revive yourself, omit the coffee and digestif. Though if you don't like late nights, you should save your dinners for Sunday evening, as I do.

Ox and Pig Cheek Stew

I love cheeks – they are emblematic of what good cooking and time can do to something hardy and unappetising: proof that there are no bad cuts of meat. This is loosely based on an Italian method for cooking ox cheeks, but the presence of pig comes from accident and making do: a Devon butcher did not have enough ox but had some pig. The two are rather different, with the pork being rather sweeter, adding a lift to the low taste of the ox.

SERVES 8

600g ox cheeks
400g pig cheeks
Seasoned flour
Olive oil
A handful of walnuts
A handful of prunes
Sea salt

Marinade
1 x 400g tin of whole tomatoes
Zest and juice of 1 orange
3 star anise
3 sprigs of rosemary
3 sprigs of thyme
1 clove of garlic
1 onion, peeled and halved
1 litre beef stock

1 stick of celery

1 carrot

The night before

1. Remove the lines of fat and muscle from the cheeks, toss them in seasoned flour and, in a large pan that can go in the oven, fry in olive oil in batches for 2 or 3 minutes on each side until browned. Set the cheeks aside.
2. Add all the marinade ingredients to the same pan, bring to the boil, then reduce the heat and simmer for 2 hours.
3. Strain the marinade into another vessel and discard the stock vegetables. Layer the cheeks in the pan and pour the marinade over. Leave to cool, then cover and leave overnight in the fridge.

On the day

4. About 6 hours before you plan to eat, preheat the oven to 120°c.
5. Put the marinated cheeks, along with the nuts, prunes and a generous pinch of salt into the oven in the covered pan. Check every now and then. If the dish is drying out, add a splash of water.
6. After 6 hours the meat should be exceptionally tender, and the sauce exceptionally delicious. Serve over polenta, with something tart and green like Swiss chard and lemon.

Sujuk Ragu with Wholemeal 'Pappardelle'

Sometime in summer and I was hungover. The fridge contained only six pork sausages and four sujuks – red Turkish sausages, made of beef, quite like spicy Spam. I really like these, even after a Turkish friend said 'You nasty' when she saw me eating them. I had tomatoes, onions and so on. So: a sauce, a bastardised and comforting thing – rich and tomatoey, a little spicy from the sujuk. I think it's best with lazily cut fresh wholemeal pasta, though a dried wholemeal pasta will do.

There's not much that can replace a sujuk – they're sold in Turkish supermarkets in almost every town and city in the UK.

SERVES 8

1 carrot, diced
1 stick of celery, diced
1 onion, peeled and diced
1 bulb of fennel, diced
Olive oil
6 high-meat-content pork sausages
4 sujuks
2 tsp fennel seeds
4 x 400g tins of whole tomatoes, mashed
⅓ of a bottle (about 250ml) of white wine
Sea salt

Pasta
400g fine semolina flour
200g plain wholemeal flour
3 eggs
100g butter, softened
100g Parmesan, finely grated

---

1. Fry the carrot, celery, onion and fennel in olive oil in a large saucepan until soft.
2. Remove the meat of both types of sausages from their skins, mash roughly with a fork, then mix the pork and sujuk and add to the softened vegetables, along with the fennel seeds. Mix everything together and fry for 2 minutes, browning the sausage.
3. Add the tomatoes, wine and a glass of water, season with salt and bring to an almost boil, then reduce the heat and simmer for 2 hours.
4. Now make the pasta. For the dough, mix the semolina and wholemeal flour with the eggs and enough water (between 100 and 200ml) so that you get a sticky dough.
5. Knead until the dough is firm and springy, about 10 minutes.
6. Roll it out lazily with a long rolling pin until thin, then cut with a knife, making rough, thick strands without uniformity.
7. After 2 hours you will have a tomatoey sauce, very thick, which you can loosen with a little pasta cooking water.
8. The pasta should be cooked until al dente in salted water, 3 minutes at most, then drained and mixed with the butter and Parmesan, creating an emulsion.
9. Mix the pasta with the sauce, check the seasoning and serve immediately.

Sunday Dinners

Dinner was exquisite, and I mean really really good. Chicken, which had been deboned and filled with light herbs, carrots Vichy, a salad from the garden and the best potatoes dauphinoise I have had. All cooked by C–, to whom cooking for nine seemed natural. It was a meal that was elegant in its apparent restraint, and was 'simple' while being rich and reliant on those two crutches (the easiest way to good cooking): butter and cream. When looking for beer, I had opened a fridge that contained only litre pots of Waitrose double cream. The chicken and the carrots were both heavy with butter, the potatoes with both; it appeared that only the salad was lacking – but no, one used that to mop up the gravy, a jus laced with cream. The genius here was that though these two pillars ('crutches' is the wrong word) were supporting the meal, they could have quite easily gone unnoticed, for everything tasted light and summery. Here we have a perfect example of Anglo-French cooking.

A Sunday dinner follows, almost exactly, the rituals of a Saturday dinner in its preparation: it is unhurried and allows the expression of creativity, since you have the whole day to cook, but comes without the expectation of liquid overindulgence. And so, since becoming sober, this is my preferred time to entertain, for I can exercise all my hostly prowess – from cocktail-making to bringing a digestif with coffee –

without my guests expecting or wishing to stay until the small hours. On a Sunday people generally leave at about twelve and rarely after one, so I invite them for seven thirty or eight, expecting to have four or so good hours of conversation before saying goodbye.

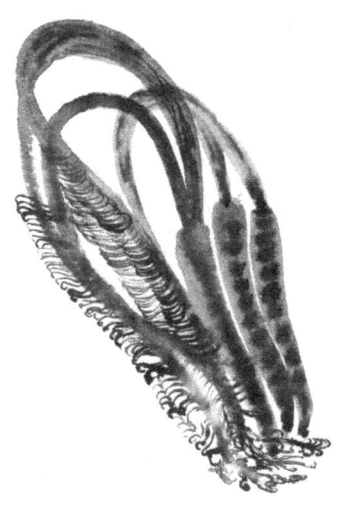

All Seasons Tart

A tart of the Devon lanes, of cycling over the hills to buy eggs and vegetables from the roadside, and using what is in season while being perfectly happy to use feta from the supermarket. The genius is that it can be made at any time of year – what stays the same is that the simple mix of cream, eggs and cheese is the base for whatever is in the house or market, roasted or blanched, and what is here is simply a suggestion. The most important thing is to get good eggs with bright yolks and to make sure you have roasted the vegetables properly, as they will not have time to cook in the oven.

If you want to add greens, like spinach or chard, simply blanch and remove as much water as possible by wringing them out in a clean tea towel. Add them to the egg and cheese mixture at the same time as everything else.

SERVES 8

1 medium butternut squash, peeled and deseeded
2 aubergines
4 courgettes
1 medium fennel bulb
3 red onions, peeled
Olive oil
Sea salt
10 rashers of bacon
A 200g block of feta
A 100g hunk of Cheddar
250ml double cream

6 eggs
A ball of Olive Oil Pastry (see page 189)
Freshly ground black pepper

---

1. Preheat the oven to 200°c.
2. Cut the vegetables rather small, put into a roasting tin and coat with plenty of oil and a little salt. Here it may be advisable to get the butternut squash in the oven 10 or so minutes before everything else, and the same for any other root vegetable you may wish to add; use your instincts. Roast in the oven until they're all well cooked and beginning to caramelise. You will probably sacrifice some to burning, but this is OK.
3. While the vegetables are roasting, roughly chop and fry the bacon in a little more olive oil in a pan until it is just becoming crispy, then set aside, keeping the fat. (You could replace the bacon with sausages, removed from their skin and broken up, the pieces fried in the same manner, or skip it entirely.)
4. Crumble the feta and roughly chop the Cheddar before mixing with the eggs, cream and a generous amount of pepper in a bowl. To this mixture, add the bacon and its fat, along with the roasted vegetables, and stir.
5. Turn the oven temperature down to 180°c.
6. This filling mixture will now get to know itself while you roll out the pastry until it is quite thin, and use it to line a large oiled tart tin (about 25 centimetres in diameter) or frying pan. Bake for 15 or so minutes until it is crispy. One ought to lay a piece of baking paper over the pastry covered with rice or something else heavy, but I sometimes skip this step since, although the pastry balloons a little, it has minimal effect on the finished dish.

7. When the pastry is cooked, remove it from the oven and pour in the tart mixture. Return the tart to the oven and cook at the same temperature for about half an hour until soft set, checking it with a knife. It is better that the egg be a little loose than dry.
8. Allow to cool for 5 or so minutes before tipping out onto a wooden board. The tart is best served at room temperature with a salad.

Sunday Lunches

Arrival was marked by the sign for the pub where my uncle worked, and after, a road entirely covered by trees, sun-dappled. The car would crunch on gravel and my grandad and granny would emerge from the front door, smiling, grandad holding a glass of wine or a small bottle of French beer. 'Hullo terrorists', he'd roar. Inside there'd be crisps on the kitchen table, wine for the adults, juice for the children, and the air would be close and hot with beef dripping for the potatoes. Grandfather, who spent his time painting portraits of the local gentry, would smell of turpentine and granny of perfume. I don't remember any of the lunches, though, just secretly thrashing at a crop of snowbells, or the sheep outside, or the trudge of boots on gravel as another guest, hopefully my uncle, approached the house.

This is the only departure from the dinner, because a Sunday lunch is worthy of special note. Sunday lunch soars with possibility: you begin in the early afternoon and have the unassigned, floating, free time of Sunday spread before you, with no obligation but to eat.

Begin with crisps and beer or white wine on the table to greet your guests, some of whom will be frowsy from Saturday's carousing. Play gentle music. Cook something big and robust: a roast, obviously, or a lasagne – any central dish whose scent fills the air. Have fun with the table: let it incarnate festivity with your best dishes and, in the winter, candles. Be unhurried. Don't overextend yourself with sides, just cook one or two vegetables – potatoes, cabbage and a gravy. I'm trying to get at the special feeling of a Sunday: leaden and at the same time free. Your guests should feel able to settle back; no one should be showing off. It's nice to have a walk after lunch but before dessert – around the neighbourhood or the nearest park – and return for crumble and custard, then coffee and sitting talking until twilight.

Slow-Roasted Salmon

This is a relaxed and simple way of cooking salmon – the flesh remains moist and sweet, the butter and herbs within turn to caramel. I was cooking a lunch for fifty in Ireland, to be transported by van from my host's kitchen in rural Tipperary to a Georgian terraced house in Dublin, so it would be cold and would have to suit the gigantic dining room. Is anything as majestic as eight kilograms of salmon? Yes: sixteen kilograms. I had two and had to break their backs and chop the longer one's head off to get them in the oven. Presenting the fish that night, I disguised this brutality with a ruff made from dill. The method works with almost any other thickset fish – trout is particularly good.

SERVES 8

250g butter
Sea salt
A whole salmon (around 2kg), cleaned and gutted but head kept on
1 fennel bulb, with stems if you can get them, roughly sliced
A bunch of sage
½ a lemon, sliced

---

1. Preheat the oven to 140°c.
2. Place the butter and a generous pinch of salt evenly in the fish's cavity, along with the fennel, sage and lemon.
3. Wrap entirely in tin foil, making sure the fish is completely sealed. Put in a roasting tin and cook in the oven for 2½ hours.
4. Serve with salad, new potatoes and a herby mayonnaise.

A Touch of Bosch

Small birds, a touch of Bosch, a gorgeous tangle, a dish to be brought to the table steaming for guests to applaud: theatre. The choice of birds is up to you: quail is white, you can eat the bones and the lightness of the flesh seems close to the texture of firm fish. Partridge is soft and supple, sweeter, with a touch of game. Pigeon seems to be of a different species entirely: the sky's beef, a gorgeous deep red, best a little bloody. Pheasant is edifying, its taste is like no other bird's, it could not be killed with anything but a gun. I first made this for my brother when, fifteen years old, he came to visit Lo' and I in our tiny apartment.

For dinner it's quite nice to have a couple of pigeons, quail, partridge and perhaps a single pheasant. Make sure the birds have been gutted, and if the butcher's left the giblets in, save them for a stock.

SERVES A SMALL CROWD

Your desired birds
Fine polenta
Salt
Butter
Sage
Rosemary
Thyme
Olive oil

1. Preheat the oven to 200°c.
2. Oil each bird, rub with fine polenta and salt, then stuff each with a large knob of butter, along with sprigs of sage, rosemary and thyme.
3. Fry the birds in olive oil in a large ovenproof frying pan until browned on each side, then transfer to the oven. Allow 10 minutes for quail, 15 minutes for pigeon and partridge, and 20 minutes for pheasant. If any look a little undercooked, throw them back in for 5 or so minutes.
4. Serve on a bed of Swiss chard, sautéed in butter and lemon until soft, and eat with a sharp knife and plenty of buttered bread for mopping up the exquisite juices.

The Dinner Before

F– goes to the top of the fridge to get more tequila and then there's the roar of the blender and she shouts that she'd learnt to make margaritas working at Vodka Revolution in Leeds before she'd become a Poet, a word she always says with a capital P. M– leans back grinning and her laughing eyes widen with love as F– places the jug on the table and, wobbly, ceremoniously, pours each of us a drink. Out of the window the warm night hurls the shouts of the Catalans and the tourists on Blai through the balcony doors.

Drinking at one of my friend's parents' houses – supermarket wine, scrumpy cider, vodka bearing the names of Soviet functionaries – was the nicest thing about going out when I was an adolescent. Handled deftly, there is a unique magic to the dinner before going out: eating together engenders camaraderie between those you'll be with all night, making a conspiratorial group, an evening's coven, formed around getting ready and, for most, getting drunk.

Serve food that balances lightness with the need to line stomachs soon to be doused in poison. Bread, cheese, cured meat and a salad, or a savoury tart. Make a long cocktail – a jug of margarita or a punch – and imagine that the actual sitting will be short-lived, followed by domestic carousing and then the sudden urgency of leaving to travel across the city much later than you'd planned. Dessert should be fleeting, to be eaten as you dash out the door to the bus or cab. Espresso martinis are good too, but for these you must make a great deal of espresso in advance and allow it to cool.

Bear in mind that evenings in London end early: pubs close at twelve, clubs at three or four, so if you're having dinner here, or in another early city, it's important to start a bit before or risk not going out at all.

How to Impress

The table was laid simply: old knives and forks, beautiful coloured plates – Italian, I think – and a few of the daffodils we'd seen outside in a jar at the centre. A plate of olives, some white sardines and a bottle of wine I knew, from my own scrimping, to be cheap. Our host said something about the casserole being ready in a bit and sat down, pouring the wine and passing the glasses, asking how our journey had been, agreeing that the trains here are much better than in England. The doorbell rang again and he rose to answer it.

If you want to impress someone, be at ease. Don't cook anything more extravagant than you would normally. In fact, do nothing you would not do for your closest friend. Crockery is hardly memorable, while a host's discomfort is. The only concession I make is who else I invite – people who make you comfortable and who will show you in a good light. It may even be good to tell them you need to appear a certain way, since people love to be co-conspirators.

Otherwise, to make sure everything goes smoothly, prioritise prepping and choose food that communicates your personality and is easy to make. If you are a neat person, able to concentrate for hours on making perfect dumplings or ravioli, then make that. If, like me, anything fiddly comes out looking like the efforts of a not quite clever child, make something rustic and easy.

A Cheap But Impressive-Looking Pie

A mushroom and beef marrow pie using meat as a flavouring rather than the centre of the meal. Equally, the recipe illustrates the way presentation can gigantically alter the feeling of a dish: the pie does not simply gain the bone marrow's flavour, but takes on a bizarre and excessive aspect.

SERVES 8

1kg mushrooms, whichever variety you can lay your hands on
Up to 300g butter
3 white onions, peeled and diced
6 cloves of garlic, peeled and crushed
2 carrots, finely diced
500ml beef and ale stock (made by dissolving 2 beef stock pots in hot ale)
1 tbsp Dijon mustard
A ball of Butter Pastry (see page 188)
3 beef marrow bones
1 egg, whisked

1. Chop the mushrooms and fry them in butter in a frying pan, in batches, until all are cooked and just turning crispy, adding more of the butter when necessary.

2. In the same pan, fry the onions, garlic and carrots in a large knob of butter until the onions are translucent.
3. Preheat the oven to 180°c.
4. Combine all the vegetables in an oven dish, along with the stock and mustard, and cook in the oven for an hour and a half.
5. While the filling cooks, roll out three-quarters of the pastry and use it to line a 25 centimetre pie dish that you have greased with butter. Roll out the rest of the pastry for the lid.
6. Remove the filling from the oven and transfer to the lined pie dish. Place the marrow bones, upright, positioned symmetrically in the dish. Cut rough panels from the rolled-out lid pastry and use them to cover the pie, arranging them around the marrow bones.
7. Paint the top with the whisked egg. Cook for 30 minutes, or until the pastry is crisp and golden.
8. Serve with lightly pickled vegetables and plenty of mustard.

Suckling Pig

A suckling pig arrives wrapped in plastic, still a little frozen. Its skin is not pink but white, a ghostly and rather tragically foetal pallor. This is meat that you can't shy away from, impolite, entirely undisguised. We needed to cook it in a couple of hours and it's a little frozen still, its legs stuck to one another, so I hold it under a tap running warmish water and loosen the legs. Again, there is the human-ness of it, but I'm strangely unaffected – a tiny quiver, which is as much a mark of respect as anything else, or a reflection of empathy; here is a whole life. I don't think eating meat is morally defensible but I still do it. Finding that it has been gutted, professionally, is comforting. Because . . . because then, obviously, this is meat, this is a carcass and, by human magic, no longer a body.

Suckling pig is like no other meat. I suppose it has the relation veal has to beef: softer, more pallid. The meat does not hold together, it's a bit like duck, though less stringy and so unlike pulled pork. Suckling pig is delicious, obscene and almost impossible to cook badly. Any good butcher will be able to order one in for you, though they can also be bought online and delivered frozen. You can add anything else aromatic to the cavity. Serve with Salad Baronne (see page 204) to cut the richness and because it adds modesty to the obscenity.

SERVES A CROWD

A suckling pig, thawed if frozen
A large bunch of thyme
1 lemon, cut into three
1 bulb of garlic, quartered

Olive oil
Sea salt

---

1. Preheat the oven to 180°c.
2. Fill the cavity of the pig with the thyme, the lemon and the garlic, and place it on your largest oven tray.
3. Rub the skin with olive oil and salt and place in the oven for 3 hours, until the flesh is buttery soft. Turn down the heat to 120°c and leave for up to 4 hours, until half an hour before serving when it should be removed from the oven and allowed to rest.

Birthdays

We didn't have many friends when we moved to London, a few from Devon and one or two from university, and we'd meet in each other's houses to cook elaborate meals. For my nineteenth birthday I wanted fruits de mer and so rose early, very early, to go to Billingsgate Fish Market, which was cheapest. It was dark as I took the bus through industrial estates and the edgelands of Canary Wharf, and mostly silent, my fellow passengers night cleaners and security guards. The quiet was vanquished as I approached the market – yelling, great metallic sounds – and with the noise came the fish smell. Inside was brightly lit with aisles of stalls holding mounds of fish, crustaceans, squid, octopus. The traders wore white jumpsuits, mostly, and white wellingtons, since the floor was horrible and wet – melted ice, mop-water and the juice of the stock. A pinkish gloss.

The shouts were communication – to each other, to customers – relaying stories, prices and many insults. The traders were mostly quite nasty, sharp-faced, wet-eyed. I wouldn't have been surprised to find scales below their ears, on their backs, and to find razor teeth in their mouths, row upon row. A star trader, the 'King of the Market', had recently been convicted of selling out-of-date fish. The customers were mainly chefs and restaurant managers, carrying out an inquisitive and efficient search, as well as a few vaguely bewildered individuals like me, asking for small amounts, met with irritation or indulgence.

I took two turns around the market, trying to keep the prices in my head to compare. I have no head for figures so never succeed, instead relying on an almost intuitive feeling, not quite memory. I bought live crabs, king prawns, oysters, mussels and scallops in their shells but baulked at lobster, which was too great an indulgence. I didn't yet like oysters, but knew they were necessary.

Outside, waiting for the bus home, an older Jamaican man asked me what I'd bought. 'Crabs, prawns, oysters . . . ' He cut me off. 'Bottom feeders! Why're you eating them? They eat the dirt of other fish.' Real Old Testament conviction, I thought, and asked, a little hurt, what he had. 'Red snapper.' And he looked away haughtily. I was glad I hadn't bought lobster.

At home I put the crabs to bed atop dishes of ice. All night I could hear their scraping movements against the wall of the fridge, slow and desperate. Lo' and I held our pillows over our heads but I could hear the scraping even in sleep. I hated it. In the morning, we took the monstrous things out – it's a happy fact that they do not have expressions, or not ones I recognise – and checked them against the size of our biggest pot. They fitted. We felt like executioners boiling the water, the crabs as helpless and still as sleeping kittens. What no cookery book told me was that they scream when you drop them into boiling water – perhaps it is simply air escaping or the contraction *of muscles. Whatever the reason, their noise is horrifying. I felt as bad as I had killing anything, worse than injured rabbits or mice. 'Hardly a birthday song.'*

A note on killing – for a long time we were told, against instinct, that dropping shellfish into boiling water was a humane way of killing them. This is not true: it causes what the RSPCA calls unacceptable levels of pain. For crabs, it now recommends 'spiking', good instructions for which are found easily online.

I have a special affection for birthdays since they're a ritual without religious or nationalist underpinnings. Neither are they concerned with achievement or success, but simply mark the passing of time and celebrate a person continuing to be.

Begin with 'So . . . what would you like?' Prod them. They might be reluctant to tell you exactly what they want, since you're cooking. Prod more. Ask what they'd had for childhood birthdays or what their favourite food is. Sometimes this will be obvious, T-bone and caviar, and at other times it will be strange, personal, like truffle and cabbage pasta. The point is to make the person being celebrated feel special and indulged. Don't overpromise – if you're making food for a large group, don't let sentiment push you away from practicality. And don't plan to make something overcomplicated or difficult that will leave you absent for the birthday, as I have many times, landing dog-tired at the table, hardly able to lift the fork, rather resenting the birthday person.

Do make a cake, or, if there are other guests who are able to, ask them. The cake, the singing of the copyrighted song, the candles: all the sacrament of this most undiscerning ritual – their absence is keenly felt, even by those who claim not to care. *Especially* by such people. On the day, double-check you have birthday candles.

If you're cooking for someone with whom you don't share money, and you're hosting their friends as well, it's perfectly reasonable to suggest they pay for everything – you can offer to go shopping with their card or ask them to bring the necessary ingredients. The former is generally best if they don't cook normally, since they'll either overspend or leave it to the last moment and get everything from the corner shop. Alcohol, too, should be their concern, though I would get a treat for them – an inexpensive magnum of wine looks the part.

Dress the table as finely as you can: this is the height of secular celebration and should be treated as such, though use nothing you will miss if it gets broken, damaged, stained. Have vases to hand if you've got them, or throw flowers into the bath.

If you're hosting at your own house, expect to be up until the celebrated wishes to sleep at least, and expect this to be late. Bring out coffee with the birthday cake and a digestif if you've got one. Put the world out of your mind. If you've cooked for them at theirs, don't be showy about leaving, and only leave if there's no chance of taking everyone else with you. On my first birthday in London, the night of the *fruits de mer*, my most glamorous guest rose to leave just after pudding, dragging all my other friends in her wake. I was nineteen and reduced to tears, their tide only stemmed after I threw a crab carcass from our window.

Lowena's Birthday Sauce

Mainly I flit in and out of conversations. And then I am boiling pasta in the biggest pot we own and telling everyone to get to the table. The room is so full and loud and exciting, and Lo' and I sit at one end on the chaise and say little, leaning into each other. I am happy to watch – everyone is content, eating, talking loudly, drinking. I want nothing more from life. It is the happiest I have been for a long while. We eat macaroni (flat sheets of pasta, so called in Barga) and meat sauce. And after dinner, more talking and smoking, more drinking – though no one gets too drunk.

Lowena's favourite food is tagliatelle with meat sauce and so I always make it for her birthday. This was a particularly good one, cooked for twenty people in our tiny flat. I have kept the amounts the same. This, and sauces in general, are excellent things to make a day ahead, as they improve from being left overnight and reheated. The sauce is not Italian, it's not really from anywhere, save my kitchen in London.

SERVES 20

2 tbsp plain flour
4 tsp dried oregano
2 tsp salt
2kg beef shin or other tough slow-cooking beef
200g beef fat (the stuff used for rolling topside; your butcher should have it)
Olive oil
100g butter

6 onions, peeled and roughly chopped
1 stick of celery, finely chopped
1 decent-sized fennel bulb, finely chopped
½ a bulb of garlic, peeled and finely chopped
6 x 400g tins of whole tomatoes, chopped
1/3 of a bottle (about 250ml) of red wine
Sea salt and freshly ground black pepper

---

1. Make a seasoned flour by combining the flour, oregano and the 2 teaspoons of salt.
2. Cut the beef and the fat into cubes, about an inch squared. Put half the fat aside and toss everything else in the seasoned flour.
3. In a large saucepan, fry the seasoned beef and fat in olive oil in batches until browned. Remove from the pan and set aside.
4. In the same saucepan, melt the butter and with a splash of oil and in this fry the onions, celery and fennel until softened. Add the garlic and continue to fry everything until golden.
5. Return the beef to the pan, stir to combine and cook for a couple of minutes.
6. Add the tomatoes, season, combine, bring almost to boiling point and add the wine. Leave to simmer for an hour, then transfer to an oven preheated to about 120°c. Leave for 7 hours, checking now and then that it's not drying out – if it is, add a splash more wine. The sauce is done when the meat is meltingly tender and the sauce slick and thick.
7. If possible, leave the sauce to cool and store it in the fridge overnight. Reheat it and serve with al dente tagliatelle.

Dinners for Lovers

It is spring, my favourite time in Devon, and when you arrive we will be able to eat in the garden beneath the crab apple tree, looking onto the hammock and the scrappy woodland below. I propose we cook outside on the first afternoon – fat little sardines bought in Ashburton from the Fish Deli, and with these fresh mayonnaise, oakleaf lettuce and potatoes boiled then tossed in mint. The mint is everywhere here, because when I was fifteen, I took packets of mint seeds and scattered them in the hedgerows and all around the garden. For breakfast, we will have boiled eggs – the eggs from the one-eyed huntress, the best in the world – with bread from the bread machine and butter made with the huntress' brother's cream. I will cut your toast into soldiers and will have mine left whole, and while you dip, I will scoop the whole egg on top. You'll have a second cup of tea and I'll have coffee, from the stainless steel pot, and we will fall asleep, again, afterwards.

Seduction is so personal that suggesting a time to invite a lover, or a potential lover, seems silly. Still, darkness is more seductive than stark light, most everyone is swayed by music and candles and confidence, and kindness and humour are appealing above anything else. A friend of mine, beautiful, boasted that their lover had brought them cheese and pickle sandwiches, and it was over these that their love blossomed.

You can sort out the light by eating late, can ensure there's music and candles, but to be pleasant you must not be stressed, and so should make nothing difficult or overly involved. Watching an able cook is thrilling and moving, quite like watching someone sing or play an instrument, and so if you're happy to be watched as you cook, have your desired sit in the kitchen with a glass of wine, with a little job too – podding peas, peeling nuts, et cetera. If you're not a confident cook, make the easiest thing you know how, something you don't need to think about. And if you hate cooking altogether, have bread, butter, good ham and cheese, with fruit afterwards.

I sent out a survey while writing this book and was surprised to find that roast chicken was the most popular suggestion for a lover's meal. Surprised not because the idea is amiss, but because it is what I myself would suggest. I think the use of hands, the simplicity, the mopping of juice with bread lends itself to that particular excitement. If not a chicken, then something else that's tactile and a little messy, that binds you with the person across the table. Steak, too, is good: the primal nature of it, its scent of flesh, exudes eroticism, especially if served with a martini. Since the meal must be light, favour fresh bread and salad over potatoes dauphinoise and buttered cabbage. Light but not puritan. If there's no excitement on your table, none will be expected from your bed.

Lamb Shoulder with Honey and Wine

This was the first dish I made for F–, my greatest cooking friend. We ate it in the garden beneath a roughly constructed calico cover, alternately protecting us from the drizzle and the June sunlight. We drank very cold Spanish white wine – something tart that offset the sweetness of the honey and cut through the richness of the lamb. It's worth making more than you'll eat, since the leftovers can be used for Roast's Ragu (see page 8).

To make the lamb described on page 12, add chilli and rose petals to the salt and honey rub, and peaches and strawberries to the apples. The rub is versatile and will accept any spices, herbs or sauces you wish to add: sumac, lavender, miso and so on. Equally, almost any fruit will do: crab apples, gooseberries, apricots, et cetera.

SERVES 6–8

1 bulb of wet garlic or ½ a bulb of dry, peeled and roughly chopped
1 red onion, peeled and roughly chopped
A sprig of rosemary
A bunch of sage leaves
4 bay leaves
A largish lamb shoulder
Sea salt
2 tbsp honey
Olive oil
4 cooking apples, peeled and roughly chopped

2 glasses of white wine
2 handfuls of prunes

---

1. Preheat the oven to 180°c.
2. Put the wet or dry garlic, onion, rosemary, sage and bay leaves in the bottom of a roasting dish and place your lamb shoulder on top.
3. Rub the shoulder with a generous pinch of salt, the honey and a glug of oil.
4. Add the cooking apples, filling the gaps left in the dish with them, not worrying if they pile up, along with the wine, a glass of water and the prunes.
5. Roast in the oven for 40 minutes, making sure the liquid does not completely evaporate, adding more water if necessary. Then turn the oven temperature down to 120°c and continue to roast for 5 hours. Check the liquid levels now and then and cover with tin foil if the lamb begins to burn.
6. Once removed from the oven, let it stand for 10 minutes and serve on polenta, with the prunes, apples and juice poured over.

Dinners for the Sick and the Sad

Some dinners will be for care rather than fun. At times in my life, I've had various people – lovelorn, broke, grief-struck, homesick, ill and lonely – over to dinner frequently, often on their own. Such dinners depart from the norm and are about concentrating as much care as possible into the food and setting – candles, soft music, a wholesome soup and cheap red wine communicate this – rather than exuberance and showing-off. There are few things more reviving than being fed, and anyone who can host has a responsibility to look out for friends who are having a bad time, especially when living in cities where so many are far from their immediate family.

Most of the time, the **lovelorn** will want to talk and to bitch. If they're drinkers, plenty should be available. You should have crisps followed by pasta, finished by something akin to ice cream (or ice cream itself) in large quantities. The ice cream is a cliché, but cliché is ritual's modern sibling, and rituals bring great comfort. Gender slips in here and asks if a man (with all the baggage and qualification that implies) wouldn't prefer the pub and sport to so much wine and conversation? Nonsense: the eloquence of heartbreak respects nothing, nor does the healing power of dessert.

Grief is based on ending, of impregnable and incomprehensible finality. Each grief might as well be the first, each is unique. After my best friend's father died, we took magic mushrooms and she saw every room in his house, then we had gnocchi and watched TV. But this is not a prescription, for none will work. Ask what might help, gently, but firm in the offer. If a grieving person has no wish to interact, do what has been done for millennia and bring them food, something contained in one dish and easily heated – a lasagne, a stew, a hearty soup. If they do come, be ready to speak a lot, or very little. The food is similar to that you'd serve someone suffering heartbreak, for grief is heartbreak without hope, but richer, grander. Truffle pasta with plenty of pepper, a steak, saffron risotto. Play gentle music, but nothing too happy nor too sombre. Offer the table or the sofa, offer a bath, offer tea, offer wine. Be responsive and not domineering.

Illness, however, can benefit from a sensitive and caring taking charge. Have someone over and say 'I will make you lemon and honey', or 'I will bring you a hot water bottle' or 'You will lie on the sofa with a blanket.' When I'm sick, this is what I desire, to be stripped of simple decisions which begin to exhaust. Importantly, however, this is not the way one should host someone who is chronically unwell, for they will be used to having their agency ignored and tend to know what they need, what they'd like. The sick ought to be fed soup with tea or water, fresh herbs, a cure-all, pear cut into slices, almonds, fresh juice, brandy and whiskey. Or milky coffee with honey, a combination recommended by a London postman when I was eighteen and answered the door of my first apartment in a dressing gown.

A Cure-All

10 sage leaves
10 black peppercorns
½ tsp fennel seeds
A finger of ginger, roughly sliced
¼ of a lemon, sliced into 4
2 tsp honey

---

1. Brew everything together in boiling water in a small pot (or a large cup) and decant after 5 minutes. Drink with a splash of cold water if it's too hot.

If someone is **too sick to leave their home**, the best thing is to bring something to them – soup travels, but so do individually packaged boxes of rice, some to be eaten now, some to be frozen for later. Gestures are wonderful, but practical help is superior, so alongside grapes and flowers, ask if the sick person needs medicine picked up or groceries bought. If they're well enough, sit with them.

Sometimes someone will simply be **lonely**. In such cases, invite them over and shower them with affection and their favourite food, set no boundaries of time and make them comfortable to stay as long as they wish. Ask what their favourite food is, and make this – loneliness often springs from a feeling that one is paid little attention, and this can be remedied by such personal consideration. If their loneliness is because they know few people, invite your gentlest and most open friends as well.

And if they know few people, it might be because they are away from home and are **homesick**. The first thing I do if someone is homesick is ask which foods they miss and how I might cook them. 'It shan't be as good as your mother's!' I'll say, for it certainly won't be, but this is not the point. Do they miss a certain hustle and bustle, a crowded table? Then a crowded table they shall have. But if they miss a quiet home, entertain them alone. The point about homesickness is not that it can be cured by familiarity, though that helps, but that it is softened by finding a new place sympathetic and lovely.

In all these cases, the most important thing is feeling the sufferer out. Are they quiet or loud, looking for distraction or wanting to examine their sadness? Be receptive and open hearted. A laptop should be welcome at the table, and dinner is welcome on the sofa or in bed. No formality should be observed and comfort must be placed at an (even greater) premium. To encourage informality, answer the door in your pyjamas or something a little slovenly, don't tidy too much. And cook together, or cook while they talk. Rid the house of nerves and expectation, be humble and offer what you can.

(Not) My Mother's Chicken Soup

This is not a soup passed down by my mother, from her mother, and so on, but something I began cooking in my early twenties, aided by various Jewish recipe blogs. The sources are lost to time, the recipe altered. It is now mine, I feel – something I make instinctively when someone I love is sick. It's worth going to a Turkish supermarket or grocer's to get the bunches of herbs: those tiny handfuls sold in plastic packets in British supermarkets are worthless. Transport the soup and the noodles separately if taking them to someone sick, otherwise they become sludgy.

SERVES 6

Soup
A bunch of dill
1 chicken
Olive oil
1 large white onion, peeled and halved
1 large carrot
2 sticks of celery
A thumb of ginger
6 cloves of garlic
A glass of white wine
1 tsp black peppercorns
1 tsp white peppercorns
1 tsp fennel seeds
5 cloves
3 star anise

1 tbsp salt
A bunch of parsley
A bunch of coriander

To finish
Baby spinach, as much as desired
Vermicelli noodles (I prefer brown rice vermicelli)

---

1. Separate the fronds of dill from the stalks, chop them finely and set them aside.
2. Roughly portion the chicken into big pieces and fry in olive oil, in batches in a large saucepan, until browned all over.
3. Take the saucepan off the heat and add all the soup ingredients apart from the fronds of dill.
4. The pan will be pretty full. Pour in enough water to cover the contents and bring to the boil, covered. Take off the lid, reduce to a low simmer and leave for 2 hours. The smell has a special effect on the sick in the house.
5. Remove the pan from the heat and take the chicken out of the stock, putting it aside.
6. Strain the stock through a sieve and return it to the original pan. You can eat the stock vegetables if you desire.
7. Let the chicken cool enough to handle, then strip the meat from the bones, adding it back into the stock. This should be pretty easy, if a little messy.
8. Reheat the soup with the chicken and add as much spinach as you desire. Meanwhile, cook as many vermicelli noodles as you want.
9. Add the noodles to big bowls and top with the soup and chicken, finishing with liberal sprinklings of the reserved dill.

Chicken and Rice for When You're Sick as a Dog

After a friend had an operation that left them almost bed-bound, and certainly too sick to cook, I made her boxes of this for her fridge and freezer. It is a simple meal that settles the mind and the stomach. For those who aren't sick, a side of salsa verde would be very suitable.

SERVES 8

1 chicken
1 onion, peeled and roughly diced
2 carrots, roughly diced
Olive oil
3 cloves of garlic, peeled and crushed
2 fistfuls of coriander stems, chopped
1 x 400g tin of whole tomatoes, blitzed
1 litre light chicken stock
A generous glass (about 200ml) of white wine
About 200g bomba or brown rice
Sea salt and freshly ground black pepper

---

1. Preheat the oven to 180°c.
2. Roughly joint the chicken with a big knife.
3. Fry the onion and the carrots in olive oil in a large saucepan until the onion is translucent. Now add the garlic and the

coriander stems and fry until the garlic is golden.
4. Fry the chicken with the vegetables for a few minutes, until browning, then add the tomatoes, chicken stock and white wine.
5. Bring almost to boiling point, add the rice and stir, then cover and move to the oven for an hour and a half, until both rice and chicken are very soft. Season to taste.
6. For those who aren't sick, this is nice with a salsa verde, but then it would be nice with many other flavoursome things the patient is not allowed. Otherwise, serve in bed or package into disposable tubs, to be kept in the fridge or the freezer.

GUESTS

It is still spring, so when the sun begins to set, everyone starts to get a little chilly and we pile into the tiny kitchen, pulling the table out. I teach Y– how to roll the pasta through the machine so that the rose petals become embedded in it, and show H– how to chop it into tagliatelle, which she does with great intensity. Lo' makes the cake in the other room, and people keep going in to visit her.

And suddenly I am boiling water for the pasta, for which I've made a mint and dill pesto, which is so green it's almost black. I am very happy when I taste the pasta and have not overcooked it, have not been distracted by the good people and drinking and music. H– plates up, again with intensity, twirling it onto the little plates. I place the lamb on a serving dish – it is blackened outside but not burnt. It is perfectly cooked: excessively tender, almost buttery. Lamb shoulder is so endlessly forgiving, so versatile. P– was naughty and put an extra pinch of chilli on it, and I was so glad they did because the spice cuts and emphasises the sweetness of the fruit, the richness of the lamb, the herbs. We pour the juice over the pasta and everyone eats hurriedly, covering their faces in grease.

After, we play 'never have I ever', which is hard because one wants to boast, and when one is so happy and fulfilled it is almost impossible to think in negatives. Then the cake is served – beautiful, thick. After that, we play 'two lies and a truth'. Nothing seems real. And then everyone is yawning, agreeing to meet again in a few days, slipping out the door, that odd feeling of sadness and pleasure at the end of a meal.

How Many?

I read that four guests are the perfect amount, 'scientifically', because with more than four conversation begins to lag, fragment and be dominated by the two most gregarious. This may be the case if each guest in the ideal four carries the conversation, if each is vocal and, indeed, interesting. But this is rare. People have partners who are dull, have bad days, then there are those who are good one-on-one but blank at the table, and so on.

Six is the best number for a group of people who know one another, and eight for a group of people you are introducing. Rarely does the humming cacophony of a well-oiled dinner – a lack of awkward pauses, a naturalness in topic – start up with a group of four, and in six this only seems to occur when everyone is on excellent terms. With eight people a continuous hum is almost guaranteed, unless your guests are very boring. You won't be talking to everyone at the same time, but you'll have had the chance to talk to everyone by the end of the evening. An important part of a good dinner is the existence of many conversations at once, and people should be encouraged to move around now and then, though I would draw the line at anything as crude as telling people to switch places. If a push is needed, show by example and steal someone's seat when they go to the toilet.

A dinner of ten is almost the same as one with eight, but any more and you'll be entering the realm of the party. Sometimes this can be excellent, but if you want to feed people well and enjoy yourself it's risky, since it's a lot of work before and stressful during the evening. Bread, cheese, meats, tinned fish and so on arrayed on a table would be the best thing for a group larger than ten – things people can eat standing.

And Who?

Spent most of the day re-writing recipes and thinking about a dinner party with F–, F–, S–, her partner, L– and someone called R–, who F– is bringing. What to cook: start with a salad of apple, celery and radicchio, then F– has bought a large fish, with which I'll make carrots, potatoes, mayonnaise and salsa verde. And finally, a piece of cake, defrosted, from NYE: a white sponge filled with sugared ricotta.

A good dinner rests on the guests, so take care with who you invite. It is important to match the personalities and interests – if one person is retiring and shy, and everyone else is loud, they may feel they can't get a word in, even if they love the same things. Similarly, at a table of retiring people, one loud person may end up seeming clownish, irritating. And for your own sanity, unless you are loud yourself, mix the gregarious with the quiet. Volume aside, I'm often excited to talk to someone who does something I know little about, so try to mix people from different worlds.

Some people tell their guests who else is coming in advance, but I don't think this is necessary – it's fun to meet someone completely new without having the chance to look them up online. But if someone does ask, don't resent this – they might be anxious or, more entertainingly, avoiding a jilted lover or someone they've brawled with.

As host, you must introduce your guests to one another. I am not a particularly shy person, but I often feel unable to bridge the unknown, so I'm touched when hosts carry out introductions. Let your guests know something or someone they have in common, from which they can build a conversation. Make sure you do this for everyone present and furnish special attention on guests who know no one.

HOUSEMATES AND FAMILY

There is nothing more jarring than sitting in someone's kitchen, enjoying the conversation, the food, when a housemate comes in and begins to awkwardly make themselves dinner. What's wrong here isn't the interruption or the noise, it's that someone in the house has been excluded from the meal, which is contrary to its very purpose. So, unless you hate your housemates, save yourself a ghost at the feast and invite them.

The same goes for your family if you're lucky enough to be taking the opportunity, afforded by high rents and house prices, to live with them. Southern Europeans are better at this, knowing that intergenerational dining is jolly. It stops their old from going off, keeps them able to hold a conversation, giving them a chance to learn from the young.

CHILDREN

The kitchen was big and airy, doors opening onto the back garden. A large table is surrounded by grownups, looking hard as rocks, so loud, their laughter explosive. Down the hall smelling of soap A–'s playroom, with its big sinking couch before a television, wide-eyed

kids – some I knew, some I didn't – all intent on the film, Babe.
It was warm and comfy and we hardly spoke.

Always ask guests with children if they'd like to bring them. Babies sleep, toddlers are silly, and pre-teens are funny and clever when playing grownup at the table. Teenagers can stay home alone so consider yourself lucky if they deign to grace you with their presence. No one should have to decide between the cost of a babysitter and seeing their friends. Think, especially, of new parents, who often feel isolated. But in thinking of them, remember too that they may be too overstretched to leave home, and will have moved fully from food as experience to food as fuel, so if you can make something comforting and filling for them, deliver it, and expect nothing in return. It is interesting that we bring food to those who have just created life and to those who are grieving, a pleasant echo in the epics of our lives.

Ask what they eat – the idea that kids are picky is foolish, they have preferences like anyone else. Besides, children's taste buds are much more sensitive than ours, rendering some things disgusting. Serve them juice as you serve their parents their wine. Ask if they'd like to sit with everyone or watch a film. Set aside a room – in our one-bed flat we use our bedroom – for them to watch a film in, letting it be theirs for the evening. Be kind and make sure they feel welcome: being a child is terrifying. If you're entertaining a few children, make them something big and easy like cheesy pasta, and find a film you loved when you were little.

I added this section late – the day before sending the book to the designer – though it's one of the most important. I'd been at lunch with the first of my close friends to have a child, in this case an astonishingly large baby called Yves, and had found immense joy eating with one hand while bouncing him on my knee.

Invitations

I almost never invite anyone with over three weeks' notice, and tend to see two weeks as the maximum. Invitations made weeks and weeks in advance tend to be forgotten, by you or the invited, or clash with more important plans that have not yet been made. I will only invite someone with longer notice if they keep turning me down because they're busy – unless I think they simply don't want to be friends – or if I know they're in high demand or travel often.

When I've invited someone, I'll remind them again a few days before – I'm always glad when someone does this for me since I'm terribly scatterbrained, though I keep a calendar religiously. It's good, too, to have a few people you don't mind inviting on the day in case of last-minute cancellations, though be careful not to make someone feel like they're only ever invited at the last minute.

Unexpected Guests

The most important thing my father taught me is that there is always enough food, and that it's a host's imperative to feed whoever turns up. Generally, I cook more than is strictly necessary, so an unexpected guest isn't an issue. Otherwise, bulk out the meal with bread, butter, pickles, anything in the fridge. At worst, a greedy person might not get as much as they'd normally have, or the balance of guests will be thrown off. All of this pales into insignificance beside the sin of not inviting someone to your table.

That there is always enough food is a maxim one should carry through life. For one thing, it's true: there is more than enough food to feed everyone on earth. It is inequality, exploitation and waste that see people go hungry – a refusal to invite people to the table.

GUESTING

We each have a role to play: a host should make their guests comfortable and a guest should be gently appreciative, entertaining and ingratiating without smarm. Such behaviour is terribly hard when people don't feel comfortable, so a bad host begets bad guests. Of course, there's no formula, save making sure to say 'thank you', and offering to help, that will ensure a person is entertaining or ingratiating – everyone will be so in their own way. So, this chapter is simply about the things my guests have done that have impressed me, and should be seen as not much more than an incomplete list.

The Golden Rule

We liked especially eating at S—'s house; she came from a family of hosts, was Iranian too. Her parents owned a vineyard and she would serve their wine, strange bottles from a Northern clime, and was generosity itself, refilling her guests' plates and glasses with alacrity, even as we sprawled happy, full and a little drunk at the edge of the tablecloth, upon cushions. Always our hands would smell a little of mint, since there would always be a plate of mint and nuts on the table. Knowing we would be so looked after, but being really up against it moneywise, we worried about a gift. And so we brought with us a pair of stoneware cups we'd been given but had little use for, made in the studio across from our tiny apartment.

Bring a wine. This is the default, for in countries where drinking is the norm, wine is as indispensable to a dinner party as the food. The cost of the wine is relatively unimportant, though I would advise a guest to spend a couple of extra pounds on the cheapest bottle of wine in a wine shop rather than a mass-produced bottle from a supermarket. It shows a little care, that the purchase had some thought. And most of the time it will be much better.

Bringing wine is important because wine is expensive – you can, with a little skill, feed eight people for very little, but – in England at least – you can't keep their cups full without a reasonable outgoing. For this reason, almost no one casually keeps enough at home to sustain a dinner party. If they do, all but the wealthiest will be quite put out to have had all their wine drunk. If you would like to be an especially nice guest, ask what's for dinner so you can choose accordingly. Champagne is always especially gratifying, while a wine of the same price is less-so, since Champagne signals celebration and only a wine pervert will know what's what. My favourite guests write to me asking what they should bring aside from wine, which is exceedingly well mannered, though I would never expect this from someone who hasn't got much money.

If your host doesn't drink, ask what you should bring. Don't be surprised if they still ask for wine. It's what I do, since I don't want to sit with a load of people who aren't used to socialising without a drink, their inhibitions unloosened. I know observant Muslims who feel similarly. For the same reasons, the non-drinker should also bring wine unless they really can't bear to buy it. Not doing so signals a certain disinterest in the other's pleasure. Obviously, some people won't want alcohol in the house – and when this is the case a gift should be obtained. As ever, be sensitive and remember your manners.

I always notice when someone makes an effort. Flowers mean a lot, especially if they're picked on the way. A fairy-like friend brought candles, black salt, black spaghetti and a wine 'that smelt like a barnyard'. A friend who tins fish brings tinned fish, even if it isn't from her tinnery, and also German bread. A painter brings beef, another, broke, brings a sketch. At Halloween we are often bought large pumpkins. If someone has an allotment, I'll hope for vegetables, if they keep bees, honey, if they make jam, jam. A baker brings bread with beautiful patterns cut into it and a friend who works in a deli brings pastries, always, and expensive apple juice. Gifts that I might not buy myself are best remembered, things unnecessary and luxurious.

If you are broke, bring something else – pick flowers, herbs, make a drawing or bring a nice object you no longer want, but think your host will like. At various times I have done all three things. And if doing so isn't embarrassing for you – *which it should never be!* – declare your penury along with your offering. It will inspire great love.

It is also undoubtedly true that I do judge the gifts I am bought according to how wealthy the guest is – those I know have little money can bring me anything (a cheap bottle of wine, a drawing) and I will be appreciative. Those I know to be in some disorder, emotional, mental and so on, can bring me nothing at all. But if someone I know to be rich does not bring a gift I mark this against them. Often, I will not invite them back. It's of note that there's an inverse relationship between wealth and generosity – I am often moved by people who have less and are thoughtful, unsurprised when those who have a lot bring nothing.

The First Time You Visit

An old friend was bringing her new – what . . . lover, girlfriend? – inamorata to dinner, to introduce her. Such meetings are important, meeting the group, an audition really, and so impressions count. She had come from L.A. and had gifts – a small painting she had made, juices and, most importantly, American cat food for our cat. Every time I think of her, a good friend now herself, I remember the touching humour in the cat food, that I remarked the next day was kind and clever and, most importantly, memorable.

Ask if you should remove your shoes. I do not like to remove my shoes – leaving childhood was proudly marked by being allowed to keep my shoes on in the house, for they were assumed to be clean, and since then I've been attached to this. However, for some people keeping shoes on in the house is disgusting – for reasons I think make a lot of sense, certainly more sense than keeping your shoes on and bringing the dirt of the street inside. Since some people are shy to ask, it's best to offer.

Otherwise, be warm and open. Comment on their home, on the smell of the food. Accept a drink. If offered a choice, state your preference rather than simply asking for what's open. People like it when decisions are made. Hand them the wine and, if it's something special, tell them what's what. If they're busy and it needs chilling, put it in the fridge. Ask for a tour, make remarks. A silent guest is spooky! If they've made a special effort with the table, notice it. Noticing is very important.

Quite often, someone who's never had you to dinner will be a little nervous – as will a new guest. But if you can, it is very helpful to do something informal and familiar – ask if you can help with the cooking by chopping or peeling, or help yourself to a glass of water. Showing yourself to be comfortable is the most calming thing you can do. But it is also hard! I felt terribly on edge in most people's houses until I was in my mid-twenties, and it was only after a lot of pretending I wasn't – helping myself to water, or fetching things from the fridge – that I began to feel at ease.

At an Inexperienced Host's

Nerves are even more apparent if a host has little experience having people to dinner, and can be quite overwhelming. It's how I felt at first. A practised guest may practise the informal familiarity opposite to quell nerves. But if things are really not going well, offering real and substantial help may be very soothing. Ask if you can stir or fry or whatever, so they can have a while among their friends, feel a little becalmed. If they're intent on remaining by the stove, take charge of the guests – make sure they're wined and watered, open the crisps, and gather them around the table. If there's no music on, sort that out. Generally take charge and give the unversed time to gather themselves.

Something I've often been roped into – almost always very happily – is helping someone to host a dinner party. This gives you, as a guest, a rather princely status and the quiet of an expectant afternoon allows you to get to know someone well. If you have a friend who you know would like to host a dinner, but is overwhelmed by the idea, offer to help, and if you have tools they lack, bring them along.

At an Old Friend's

J– is coming for a walk and carries the mix of humour and magic for which she is adored, and from a bag removes a bottle of red wine, a packet of squid ink spaghetti, a truffle salami, a bar of Italian soap called Black Cock, two beeswax candles and a packet of black salt – to sprinkle where one's enemies tread, so that they do not reappear.

Not instructional at all, but isn't it wonderful to eat somewhere you've eaten often before, with someone you are truly comfortable with? You assume a sort-of premier status, can open cupboards at will, serve wine and lean back in your chair, happy in community. I'll ask old friends if they'd like me to bring something, and will find out what would be truly useful. If you'd like a chat with them before everyone else arrives, ask to come a little early. Answer the door and seat the others. Choose the music.

At a Host's Who's Broke

F– rings the bell, laden with bags, and says she'll have to go back to help G–, so I go too, picking up a box of wine: he has many bags and a magnum in one hand. There is the exciting rush of hellos and kisses and we are in the kitchen, bags everywhere. Unpacked are: two cakes, one from F–'s mother, that very light Chinese sponge with cream, topped with kiwi, strawberries and mango, and another, from a friend, iced with very shiny chocolate icing. There are six bottles of wine, a bottle of whiskey, a bottle of rhubarb vodka and the magnum: the wine is all very beautiful, 'chosen because I thought the labels would make you happy, Lo'. There are two côtes de boeufs ('twice as much as we had on New Year's Eve, but for half the people!'), crackers and cheese, a bag of potatoes, butter. It is a feast: in G–'s words, we went ham tonight. G– and I cooking, G– calling the women our rulers and trying to explain his work to me . . . and my never understanding nor, I suppose, listening attentively enough. We seal the meat and cook it in a hot oven, alongside dauphinoise, made with a tremendous amount of butter and cream. Eating, Lo' says she would like one day to write about the taste of good beef's juice, this stuff being particularly wonderful, augmented with butter and flavoured by thyme and rosemary.

We were always the hosts – we'd feathered our nest as best we could, and I knew how to cook – but were commonly without a penny. Less regularly now, but this is still sometimes the case. Good friends would bring us everything for dinner, and I'd cook it as we chatted, content in something that wasn't an exchange but a show of mutual appreciation. So, if you know someone wants to host but isn't flush, and you are, ask if they'd like you to bring the meat, the wine, the cheese or everything together. If they refuse, bring plenty of treats, expensive things they wouldn't buy themselves. And be appreciative – for one host's simple pasta can have the weight of another's caviar.

Lateness and Cancellation

It's nice to let your host know if you're going to be more than half an hour late. It is very un-chic to arrive exactly on time, especially if you don't know your host well. The only time you should arrive *early* is if you've asked your host and they've said yes, or if you commonly share a bed – romantically or otherwise. If your lateness reaches over an hour, have a good excuse, and tell everyone to start without you. Always add five minutes to your arrival time, so that you're a little earlier than you've said – a nice surprise rather than the irritation (some) feel if someone arrives even later than they've said.

Cancelling is always difficult. It would fill me with pangs of guilt and fear when I was younger, and still always feels difficult today. But rest easy in the knowledge that it rarely matters as much as you'd think. What matters is telling your host as soon as you know and not lying – it is much better to receive a message saying you're just not up to dinner, for whatever reason, than something spurious. If you are going to lie, only ever use one excuse and do not be profusely apologetic – someone who has a genuine ailment rarely feels the need for ten apologies, but a liar does.

THE ROOM AND THE TABLE

There was a bath in the kitchen. 'Have you used it?' 'It doesn't get hot water.' Now it was covered with a board which held a dying plant and a stack of pots and pans. They didn't have a table, so had placed a cloth over two pallets – 'Careful of the gaps!' The cloth was from the flea market, stained and of once-expensive cotton, thick, tightly woven. I put my glass down in a gap and it spilt. 'Oh no, in the gap!' And then squawks of laughter. The old cat glowered and I ran to get a cloth but was shouted down, so sat back onto my cushion.

Making a Dining Room

Most of us don't have a room just for dining. Currently, aside from a small bedroom and tinier bathroom, our flat is all one largish room. In adulthood I have only once had a dining room – this in a leaky house, quite dark, in the suburbs. But I have always been lucky enough to have somewhere – wedged in a galley kitchen, dominating a studio apartment – to have a table set up. I feel quite lost without a table to eat at, and while Lo' is rarely more comfortable than when eating in bed, I find the experience sweaty and reminiscent of illness.

Many don't have the luxury of a permanent table: our flats are too small, our landlords turn what might have been a dining or sitting room into another bedroom. The exorbitant cost of rent has left many with little ability to show regard for communal space. A house with an orange door, where I had my fondest university dinners, had the dining table wedged into the corner of the small kitchen. To get to one side one had to crawl beneath it, but this hardly mattered. It uncomfortably sat six, and often eight.

If a flat has a sitting room but not a room with a table, I'd choose a table over a sofa. But preference can't serve as advice. So, if the sitting room is not primarily somewhere for eating, I would buy a folding table for dinners and have it folded away the rest of the time. I find it especially touching when someone creates a place to eat where there isn't one normally – it shows a lot of effort and care. Don't worry too much about chairs, though the folding chairs from Ikea – the first chairs we ever owned – are fine and don't take up much space. Equally, pulling soft chairs, a sofa, stalls, office chairs, even packing boxes, to a table is fine; rather chic actually. Sofas especially leave one feeling a touch Roman. In bedrooms, if there's space, use your desk as a table, or bring a trestle in. As long as you make your bed and put your clothes away, this is perfectly lovely.

A CLOTH FOR A TABLE

If you don't want to use a table, or don't have one, lay a cloth on the floor. This manner of eating, common around the world, was called an 'inside picnic' when I was a child – an important thing growing up in a wet country, where outings are often rained off. Treating eating on the

floor as frivolous would be a mistake: one of the most beautifully laid dinners I've been to was thrown by an Iranian friend of mine who had set a cloth (a *sofra* in Farsi, with similar names in Arabic and Turkish) with an ornate mix of Persian and European dishes, candelabra, plates and glasses. Most westerners are used to eating at tables, but there is nothing about the object itself that blesses a meal; rather, its importance lies in making guests look at one another, and thus talk, and in marking the space between the world of food and the world outside food. A cloth has equal power. If you have them, cushions do well for replacing chairs, though one needn't spend the whole meal sitting up. Everything said about table setting later applies here.

In Praise of Small Rooms

An issue most of us do not have, but may occasionally come across, is choosing the size of a room to eat in. Luckily, the rule here is democratic – smaller rooms are better for getting on, they encourage laughter and get rid of constraint. Large and empty rooms can leave you feeling unmoored from the other guests. Eating rooms ought to have windows – just as important at night, when there is comfort in the dark outside behind a pane of glass and a good air flow.

Theatre

We have the most lovely time, drinking Champagne, then good wine, then elderflower champagne – the best I've ever had. F– shows me how to cook rice in the rice cooker – rinsing it with casual expertise ('this rice doesn't have so much starch on it . . . ') then showing me that she measures the amount of water by one knuckle. She becomes an adept cook, throwaway and busy. The stew is delicious, light and sweet, and sits tremendously well with Champagne: a new pairing, Champagne and pork belly stew.

Dining ranges from an intimate to a grand performance – either way, your table, its cloth, your glasses and plates, and the flowers, are props and should be chosen with care. An overly formal setting will alienate most people – it's sort of tacky too – and an ugly setting will detract from the care you've put into the food. Of course, there are situations when these rules don't apply, since, like all rules, they're rather silly.

I did not, for instance, feel as uncomfortable as I might in a grand house in Dorset where each guest had their own silver salt and pepper cellars. For dinner we had a simple, and actually rather mediocre, omelette and green salad, with a bar of chocolate shared around the table for dessert. Equally, there was great charm in the cheap tin cutlery and violently clashing chinaware – some from Ikea, some from the nineteenth century – at a friend's childhood home in Lazio. There the food was unsurpassed and the clean air, after Rome's fumes, ambrosia.

But, a most important note: when I talk about the minimum or optimum number of things, I don't expect anyone to have everything, or to rush out and spend a great deal of money. My advice should be taken as a Utopian goal, rather than a necessity for starting out, and reflects my own possessions, which have come together after a decade or so of finding, smashing and finding again, trawling markets, charity shops and eBay. Importantly, these goals are mine too: I don't have enough bowls at the moment and I am in dire need of wine glasses. I want to stress, again and again, that if people see that you have put care into a meal, they will find that almost nothing else important.

Laying the Table

After the girls go out, I hear, every now and then, an odd electric-sounding whistle. An alarm, maybe, or a loud phone? I ignore it for a while, as I had ignored the clanging of gas canisters as the gas men roll them up and down the street precariously balanced on dollies. Hanging out laundry, I see that the whistle belongs to a knife grinder, the second on the street this week. This one's machine is a large wheel attached to a foot pedal, as on a manual sewing machine; last week's was attached to a small motor harvested from a scooter. This week's is more picturesque, though last week's had a nicer-sounding whistle. I pack the knives in a tea towel and wander downstairs and present them. He nods, mumbles something, takes them, touches them with his hands, assesses, turns them over and one by one runs them over the quick-spinning flint. His is a practised concentration, an effortless sort of focus, unhurried, unworried, moving gently out of the way of people passing him on the pavement without ceasing his wheel. A woman asks him how much he costs. It depends, he says, three, four, five, six. After he has finished with the wheel, he takes a whetstone from a sheep's horn tied to the machine, gives what look like cursory, customary, superstitious dashes to the blades. And after, his final theatre: he removes a small spiral-bound notebook from his pocket, removes a page from this, and with each knife makes sharp short gentle slices, *not looking at me. I feel happy and calm, almost for the first time in days, watching with the sun on my back.*

Should we lay the table before the guests arrive? It was how I would do it when I first began hosting. But a little later I began to dislike doing so, feeling it spelt a certain formality, even self-consciousness. So I began letting people sit down – I would shoo them around the table and would wait until food was almost ready before tossing plates, knives and forks, a stack of glasses, a jug of water. It felt informal and confident. Recently this has begun to chafe against a part of me that likes to set the tone, that misses ritual. So I've started to do it again, and enjoy laying the table, carrying to it the objects we've spent years finding. Guests gravitate to a laid table like moths to light.

Tablecloths

My mother kept our tablecloths in an ottoman at the foot of my parents' bed, to be fetched for special occasions. Otherwise, the kitchen table was covered with a wipe-clean oilcloth, changed when it became stiff with age.

Tablecloths are objects of ritual – they elevate and move the table from a surface to a site of incantation. If I could, I'd have tablecloths at every meal, though if I did they'd lose their significance. But since washing them is a drag – especially if, like me and unlike my mother, who may have a better washing machine or be a witch, you can never get the stains out – I reserve them for special occasions. Worrying too much about the weight of the cloth or the colour, however, is a mistake. A bed sheet will do!

My mother's were of different colours and patterns. My favourite was from India, bought when visiting my brother's godparents in Delhi, and was white with flowers on it. Mine are all plain white, since I like the severity of a blank surface beneath the bright colours of dinner. But you must choose prints or florals or nothing at all to suit your own taste, for taste is not prescriptive but an expression of the self.

Lighting

It is tragic when a dinner is spoiled by too-bright light! Your guests will be kept on the edge of their seats, oddly alert, and will never fall into the near-somnambulance that accompanies really good conversation. When they get drunk to escape the glare, they will become aggressive and mean-spirited. Unless your electric lights have dimmers, buy lamps or candles and candlesticks, and create a light that is not dark – that will make everyone sleepy – but is comfortable and flattering to the food and guests.

Dinner is a ceremony and ceremonies have their physical manifestations, their robes, scents, lights. Many of us no longer visit temples and so more keenly miss their trimmings. Candles hold their own importance and the light they cast contains enchantment. Moreover, they are a relatively cheap way to bless an otherwise un-made table with a sense occasion.

Also, they make everyone look a great deal more beautiful, and provide a primal feel to the table. I go for off-white taper candles on quite simple candlesticks, but candles in wine bottles are as charming, of any colour. Putting candles on a table is a great example of the important fact that trying to create beauty goes a long way and is often all that's necessary.

Flowers

Flowers, too, lend ceremonial significance and they gesture at that other thing about ritual, the elevation above necessity. They bring the outside in and grant dinner a little of nature's elegance. In summer, they can replace candles and become their own jewels.

If I have a large bunch of flowers, in a jug, say, I will remove it before everyone sits to eat, since it will get in the way – of the food, yes, but more importantly of people looking across the table. If you want your flowers to remain during eating, make small arrangements in unobtrusive vases, jars, glasses – the vessel doesn't matter – that don't block the view.

Music

Unless you know there will be conversation without pause, music is a necessity since silences at the table, as guests cast around for something to say, can feel terribly awkward. The music ought not be too loud, and should be light on words or in a language the guests cannot understand. Mostly I play jazz, which is perfectly suited to be in the background, having been designed to be played in nightclubs. For this reason, most secular eighteenth-century music is great too, since it was played to groups dancing and talking.

One of the oddest pieces of advice I received when I began writing this book and asking people for hosting tips was to have two sources of music: one in the room where people were assembled and another in the toilet. I have never taken this advice. What I do recommend, however, is attaching the speaker to anything but your phone – it is irritating when it stops because you need to make a phone call or take a picture.

Serving Ware

In my early twenties I began loathing bringing saucepans to the table, finding so few that were both beautiful enough and practical. I've calmed down about this, but harbour a love of presentation – a chicken on a large board, beef on a metal platter, cheese on a pewter charger.

I think it is good to have one or two large oval serving platters and a few that are smaller for salads and so on. Carrying a large laden platter to the table lends an element of theatre: it concentrates diners' minds. But there's really nothing wrong with bringing the saucepan. I do tend to present vegetables and various sides on nice plates, elevating sundry dishes to their rightful position of importance.

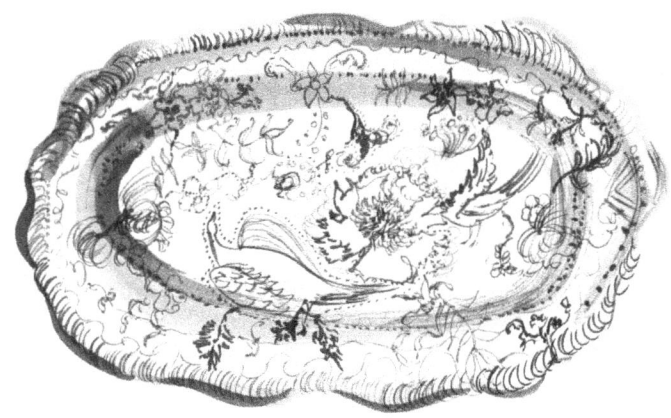

Cutlery

Bone-handled knives – the yellowish sort – and metal forks are my favourite, because there is a happy contrast between the feel of bone in your right hand, warm and organic, and cold metal in your left. They're also unfashionable and can be picked up reasonably cheaply at most antique markets – there is a wonderful old man who specialises in cutlery at Spitalfields Market in London on Thursdays, for instance. Weighty metal cutlery is nice in the palm, but tends to be expensive, even second-hand. Modern cutlery, bought new, can be perfectly nice, but costs a great deal and this seems a shame when the old stuff is so easy to find and relatively cheap.

I would not worry about cutlery matching, though it is certainly nicer if everything is of the same general type. What one should avoid, though, are the fiddly specifics of the Victorian table – soup spoons, fish knives, cake forks. All you want are chopsticks, forks, knives, table and teaspoons. Everything else seems designed to fill the time of young men and women forced into service, not only in the nineteenth century, but in the fast multiplying houses of the modern rich. It is for this reason that I dislike silver generally, since its proper and gleaming presentation is used to illustrate the extent of a house's staff, silver taking so long to polish.

Plates

Your plates need not be expensive, antique or of a set, but it's nice if they roughly match in size and colour. A good minimum is eight or so dinner plates, and the same number of small plates for desserts and bowls for noodles and soup. The same rule goes for plates as for knives and forks – they are so much more expensive new, from a high street shop, than they are from a market or charity shop that unless you're really stuck for time, or have a real love for them, they seem a waste.

Glasses

After lunch, rest, and after rest we march off to the flea market in Encants – the Enchanted Market – and there Lo' is like a ferret and I become a machismo haggler. A couple of beautifully carved hands, a saint's, chipped and broken, are eighty euros. I roll my eyes and we look elsewhere, at some brass ribbons – the sort for decorating a door. As I look at these, the man lowers the price of the hands to forty. Oh, so this is the game. Ten for the ribbons, I say, two-fifty each seems fair. No! Twenty! No. Lo' offers fifteen and I brush her away. No. Ten. I turn to leave. OK, ten. I offer twenty for the hands but the man shakes his head and we leave. This is bartering – real bartering where you cajole and insult, not the sniffling English kind. Lo' goes to a store selling linens. A large, thick, beautiful sheet, which in Bologna – at a fancy stall, cleaned and pressed – costs sixty is, says the holder, eighty. I laugh, he laughs and says forty. No. Twenty. No. thirty. He writes it on his phone. The last price. No, twenty. No! Twenty-five. OK, twenty-five but throw in the top. He grins and assents. Asks where we are from. London. Oh, amazing. And him? Bangladesh. Where in Bangladesh? Dakkar. Oh, city boy! We laugh, compliment each other's countries. Alone, I go back to the hands. Twenty-five. No, forty! OK, I'll go, I turn to leave. '30', written on the phone. I delete it and write '25'. No! I turn to leave again. OK! At another stall – linen bloomers and a linen cape, both nineteenth century, but in imperfect condition. Thirty for both, a deal! Hahaha, I laugh, loco! Maybe in the mad house. He mocks annoyance. I say ten. He says thirty. I turn, it becomes twenty. I insist, he insists, I turn again and it becomes ten. He grins and thanks me as I hand him the money. I am on fire, almost trembling with the exertion of not being mild mannered and kind, and all this communication with arms and telephone screens, with so few shared words.

I love beautiful glasses, but glasses break. So I don't spend much money on them, but scan charity shops and markets for interesting specimens, get quite used to them – arriving in sixes, threes, twos – and try not to get sad when their time comes. The nice glasses live on a shelf and come down for special occasions, otherwise Duralex are the best, one size for water and a smaller one for wine. Ten of each are all that's necessary. As long as your guests have something to drink from, they won't care.

Furniture

I see collecting kitchen furniture as a long up-hill clamber. At the moment our kitchen table is a wobbly extendable thing of a dark veneer, inherited from a friend when they left London years ago. I don't like it, but it serves its purpose. Our chairs are mostly my brother's, left with us while he lives an errant life. Alongside these a desk chair, which Lo' upholstered with rough linen, and a heavy wooden bench. When the need arises we bring to the table another, flimsy bench, which I made, and of which I am inordinately proud.

This marks great progress. When Lo' and I first moved in together we had no furniture save a futon, on which we still sleep. It was nine months or so until we got Ikea chairs, which I carried from Vauxhall to Shoreditch on the bus, on my shoulders.

What I'm saying is, don't worry! Furniture is really expensive and there's something suspicious about people who have everything too young. Either they're too successful or you should ask what, exactly, their parents do. Plates, knives and so on are small, fun to collect, inexpensive to buy and they can be what you rely on for self-expression, and I hope good furniture will come with time.

Charity Shops

Regardless of what I've recommended above, when you're beginning to host, all you need are the bare bones. These bones will be cheaply available from any charity shop: enough glasses, cutlery and plates for each guest you wish to invite. Wildly clashing, half horrible, it hardly matters as long as you receive people with grace and excitement. And feed them well.

I asked if she had any sheets. 'No . . . well, some have come in but they're not priced yet.' She looked apologetic. 'The manager has to price them.' A touch of resentment here. 'Oh, but I need one . . . I don't have one.' Morally true, I think. I don't have a tablecloth . . . Apology turns to pity in her eyes, and pity to a revolutionary solidarity. 'Oh well, if you're desperate I don't see why I have to wait for her.' She goes into the crowded room behind her, quick, ferret-like among the donations, and returns, thin cotton sheet aloft. 'Three pounds!' I thank her, thank her again, and pay with three pound coins.

WHAT TO MAKE

We were staying beside the Dordogne – the river swishing past the house snakily slow, the country around mostly quail farms, the tiny birds squawky and less noble than chickens. One day we drove up country to visit the Baronne D– F–, the mother of another guest who'd told us, shyly, that her mother's home wasn't a house but a château. 'Maman is haughty, but it is a beautiful place and she will give us a good lunch.' No matter one's politics, titles still inspire a little trepidation. I suppose they're like churches, which possess a feeling of awe whether one believes or not, no matter the evil committed in their name. And so we were all a little shy and dressed as smartly as we could. Hard for me since most of my clothes were in tatters or dirty, as I'd packed for a week of cooking and swimming and had been wiping my hands on my trousers.

The château was indeed beautiful – a large arch, barred by a thick oak door, into a courtyard, on one side the house, its various architectural styles showing its age, on the other side a small park and riding sheds. The baroness looked like any other rich French woman: tightish jeans, a gilet, well-coiffed hair and a pink Lacoste cigarette holder, from which she produced a near constant stream of Dunhills. After we greeted her in very broken French she replied, sharply, that she did not speak English. This was modesty or a joke, for she spoke

English eloquently as she showed us round the rooms – most of which were deserted and in disrepair, the family having retreated to a dwelling the size of a townhouse rather than a palace. The château had been in her family since the sixteenth century, save a few years when it was requisitioned by the revolutionary government. 'They broke lots of things' – said as if the sans-culottes had stormed the Bastille in the last decade, expecting a sympathy we did not have.

In the sitting room – cosy, rather dark, quite stuffed – we drank Champagne, served by the baroness's son who was in the midst of getting ready for his first debutante ball. 'Remember, the female guests first, then the male guests – oldest first, though only if someone is obviously older, don't ask – then your sister, then me, because I am the hostess, and finally you. But if I were not the hostess, me first since I'm the eldest.' The boy nodded, pouring as his mother spoke. A little later the baroness clapped her hands, 'Wake up! Your guests have empty glasses!' He jumped up from the chair in which he had been slouched, very bored. Later, we saw that his bedroom contained a gaming computer and a remote-controlled helicopter.

Lunch was in the kitchen, which, the height of its ceilings aside, was like countless other posh kitchens in a French country style: pleasantly painted, an Aga on one side, with a large farmhouse table. The table was already set, simply, with plates, napkins and wine goblets, which the baroness must have done before we'd arrived. 'Now, a simple lunch!' On the table, baguette in a basket, white butter in a dish. The wine was simple, too, but very good. Our first course was coarsely cut red cabbage dressed in vinegar and wholegrain mustard; and after, roast chicken with roast new potatoes and jus in a little white jug. After that, two local cheeses with the baguette, and a great deal of laughter as we were taught the proper way to eat cheese: not to place it on the baguette but to cut a slice, straight not diagonal, and take a bite from it and then from the bread. This seemed utterly obtuse, almost *barbaric, but we did as instructed. The baroness, now happy, skipped down to her cellar to fetch two bottles of bright blue wine, called Vindigo. Drunk, holding our glasses, she took us out to her garage, and bade us drive her MG ('my English car') around the walled garden.*

It is no exaggeration to say this was the best roast chicken I have ever eaten, and the jus was superior to any I have ever made, but that is not the point. While I remember the rickety stairs and the ramparts on the highest tower, I remember with greater intensity the elegance of serving red cabbage and nothing else as a starter – a sincere lack of showiness has never left me. The salad wasn't even that good, but that was part of it. Each stage of the lunch was executed with a spectacular theatricality – not the obvious theatricality of musical or opera, but the theatricality of a play that one forgets is a play, where stagehands are entirely unobtrusive and the actors could be people at another table in a restaurant.

I like telling this story because there's a joke in it, of how silly it is to claim one has learnt simplicity from a chatelaine. As we drove back, I complimented the baronesss' daughter on her mother's skill as a hostess, how natural everything seemed, how perfectly timed and discreet. 'Well, yes, of course. This has been her career, being a hostess, so I'd hope she'd be good.' Her daughter told us how her mother had described us: Lo' was extremely elegant and I, she assumed, an aristocrat. I told her that my people would have been with the *sans-culottes* raiding the château.

At the most general level, regardless of occasion, two things govern what to cook for a dinner party. The first is what you have the means to produce, not only financially, but what you can do with relative ease and enjoyment; the second is the preferences and needs of your guests. But there is a third, related to the second: do not forget yourself. It is not possible to cook something you do not like with grace. Everything about the aristocracy should be destroyed, save one thing: the comfort they have in their preferences. Such comfort should be democratised and felt by everyone.

Money

When we began to have people to dinner in our little studio flat, I would think all week about the cost of ingredients, and would travel to the cheapest fishmonger I knew to buy king prawns for a pasta I was particularly fond of. Enough for six people, for five pounds! The place was always busy and, since those customers weren't getting ill, I did not think I would. I was right. Sadly that fishmonger is no more. I would take the bus across town to the closest Lidl and fill a most gigantic bag up there and lug it home with me, looked on piteously by the women on the bus. I would scrimp and save, totting up the difference between the cooking chocolate in Sainsbury's and Tesco, and might spend another hour shopping to ensure I saved ten pounds.

It was a lot. Hard work. But it meant I never felt I'd overstretched myself, never felt providing food for people was beyond me, never touched on resentment. I am lazier now – and no longer a student, mad with energy and time – but the spirit of making food, everything really, with what I can comfortably afford has not left me. And it has taken on a shine of its own: for through this I have developed a rejection of unnecessary expense and a firm knowledge that good food, good things, creativity even, come not from easy gratification but from the clever use of what is available. And my guests would heap my simple pastas, my pizza topped with roast vegetables, my pestos made with the cheapest herbs and nuts, with praise. It is a lack of time, rather than an excess of money, that has put a stop to such questing.

Italian food, splendid and varied, is at its roots a cuisine of peasants and the urban poor. *Cacio e pepe*, the most Roman of dishes, is formed from a little cheese but, most importantly, the emulsion of water and starch. Pizza is a thin dough spread lightly with tomato and graced with a little mozzarella. Meat and cheese are rarely found together. Such simplicity is not because of the Italian soul, but comes from sparsity. This we can see when the Italian poor had as much food as they could eat and created spaghetti and meatballs, Chicago pizza and the Milanese, a cutlet of veal deep-fried with cheese and ham.

I am not fetishising not having enough – without a great deal of time and energy my student scrimping would have been hellish, part-time job that it was. But it does show that you don't need to spend a great deal of money to entertain well. If you have a candle, two candles, and serve spaghetti with tomato sauce and then pears that you yourself have sliced, you have looked after your guests and will be remembered for doing so. It is fun to indulge, it is fun to play with luxury, but it is nothing next to an egg, lovingly peeled, served with bread and butter. So, yes, means do dictate. They create limitations and borders and problems to solve, but they ought not prevent you, if you have the time and the energy, from hosting.

On a practical level, this might mean being strict about what you make, knowing what you can and can't afford. It may mean asking your guests to pick up the more expensive things on the way – I often ask people to bring Parmesan – or to bring dessert. Worry about food before alcohol, and if wine is too much, get beer. Never buy something that's so expensive you resent it, and if you ever do do this, never tell your guests.

What do I remember eating as a child? A memory I can taste is hoppers with a fried egg in them and the almost sweet and not at all spicy green banana curry my father would make. There was one lunch, everyone was eating in the garden, on the patio. I was sitting, maybe, with my knees up or feet dangling over the step with a tin bowl of the light green curry, avoiding the curry leaves which got stuck in my teeth, and alternating between the halves of long new potatoes and the green bananas. The former were a disappointment but the bananas were unique in their sweet–savouriness, and among all this was a piece of chicken, a leg or a thigh, salty and juicy with a satisfyingly slippery skin. The hoppers were even more special, their brown crispy outside and the powdery batter, white, pockmarked with air, quite like a crumpet. Beside it was a sambal, a worrying dry spicy sort of chutney that I could not stomach but now eat most breakfasts. The day was warm and I heard my mother tell a friend that the man who had done the patio had stepped in front of a train. What an odd thing to do, I thought, wandering around later, my mouth sweet from coconut milk.

A Sort of Ratatouille

This is the result of hundreds of bastardisations. The first, I think, came from a food-encrusted Delia Smith book, and was cooked when I was fourteen. Since then, it has served many guests, its continued use testament enough.

SERVES 6

4 aubergines
Olive oil
6 courgettes, sliced
2 red onions, peeled and sliced
6 cloves of garlic, peeled and crushed
4 x 400g tins of whole tomatoes, blitzed
Sea salt

---

1. Halve the aubergines lengthways, then cut into inch-thick slices. In a large saucepan, fry them in batches in plenty of olive oil until soft and golden, then set aside. Then fry the courgettes until softened but still retaining a crunch, and set aside.
2. Fry the onions and garlic over a medium heat until golden. Add the tomatoes, bring to the boil, then reduce to a simmer.
3. Introduce the aubergine and courgette along with a generous pinch of salt and cook on a simmer for 40 minutes, stirring occasionally, until the sauce has thickened and taken on a sweetness.
4. Serve with rice, couscous or polenta.

Kitchen

As it is important to consider what you can afford, it's important to consider your kitchen. When I cook in my current flat, with a landlord-issue electric oven that can't keep a consistent temperature, topped by coil heat pads, this is as key to my decisions as the ingredients. I cannot flash fry; I could not trust it to make soufflé. I put water for pasta on to boil fifteen minutes before I'll need it and know I can only run three hobs at once. Whenever I think something will be OK, think my skill great enough to overcome the kitchen's failings, I'm overwhelmed: a cake won't rise. I curdle the custard. Overcook the capon. The overcooked capon happened at Christmas and brought me very close to tears.

Working out what your kitchen can do takes a little time, but there are some useful questions, which I've learnt to ask when doing a site visit before a commercial dinner. How much can you fit in the oven? How big are the pots? How much workspace is there? How many knives? How hot is the hob? Are there enough mixing bowls to use and put dirty to the side, or will I need to wash the only one after each use? Overestimate what you'll need!

Ability

It would be silly to hold yourself to the example of a restaurant or dinner parties of yore. Restaurants have a team of trained individuals and the twentieth-century dinner party, with its fussiness and multiple courses, relied on women who, like my grandmother, gave their day over to labour. To make cooking fun, you must see that it is work, and that such work must be respected.

First, what can you do with ease? If you've always struggled to make mayonnaise, don't make it. If, like me, you seem unable to bake, buy fresh bread. Second, how much time do you have? If something takes two hours to make, and there's two and a half hours to make it, make something else: well-executed simplicity is superior to poorly executed complexity. It's not so much that your guests will care, it's that *you* will.

Diet and Preference

Ask if there's anything your guests can't, or won't, eat – asking for dietary preferences avoids someone not eating the food at all, or, worse, eating it without enjoyment. I used to think it was the guest's responsibility to explain their dietary requirements, but I take a much gentler position now – it can feel like an imposition to tell someone who's already cooking you dinner that you don't eat something, whether because of taste, morals or health. Since a host's role is a gentle one, aiming to avoid unease, making space for your guests' needs is of the utmost importance. Only then can you create Utopia.

Most of the time it is best to cook a dish that everyone can eat – making someone their own dish, however kind this is, can be added work. If cooking something entirely bereft of a particular ingredient is impossible – replacing the joint or bird from a roast dinner, for instance – it is then a host's responsibility to make a dish to replace it. If you are very skilled and have a lot of time, this might be an expansive dish, but if you're not, simple is perfect. Even if what you make is mediocre, the guest will be touched that you've made something specially for them and won't notice. The food is not the point.

Research and Reverie

After you've established what people can eat, you can have fun.

It might begin the day before, or two days before. At my desk I will start to think – Saturday. Well, there is the sweetbread in the freezer, so I can deep-fry that. It needs to be taken out on Friday, though. And there's a vegetarian coming, so I shall make a main without meat. And there will be eight or ten, so something simple and filling. I have not made gnocchi for a while and ought to use a recipe book to refresh myself. I take one from the stack beside my desk and thumb through *The Essentials of Classic Italian Cooking* by Marcella Hazan, a bible. After reading the recipe for gnocchi I read a recipe for a paired sauce – tomato with onion and

butter, the 'simplest of all sauces to make'. It is so simple, entirely unlike how I make sauce – leave the onion in half and discard after an hour's cooking. Research leads to reverie, to an expansion of the cooking imaginarium, hinting at new departures.

How to Cooperate

Bone marrow cooked over rosemary, which we eat with a caper and coriander salad and toast in the dining room, the four of us at one end of a table that would seat four times as many. The room is lit by three candelabra, a line of candles in front of a large mirror and the chandelier, its bulbs dim. C– is pleasantly greedy. The marrow is very good; with it we drink martinis made from a vodka that has a glass dragon inside its bottle and is laced with gold flakes, a well-dusted and untouched birthday gift. We return to the kitchen to make a squid ink spaghetti, with a sauce of its own ink, an idea the Italian finds terrible. This is something wonderful about British cooking: it has no cuisine to look back on, no grand traditions – no rules, really. F– is even less bound by European tradition than I, which comes from his astounding arrogance, and this is mostly positive. We are jealous of the Italians, but the last time they were allowed to make anything new was the turn of the nineteenth century; contemporary Italian cuisine is either a practice of greater rusticity or deeply influenced by International Cooking. F– is the only person I really enjoy cooking with: we trust each other, but know we make mistakes. I over-salt, he adds too much lemon. We are watchful in the way jazz musicians are watchful, individuals who form something together.

Sometimes you'll be hosting with someone who you don't share a bed with, and this can expose patterns of dominance you didn't know existed. It may also show how well-calibrated your friendship is. If such patterns emerge with whoever you do share your bed with, you ought to know them better.

Most of my friends defer to me when we cook together, and I've come to accept this and give them tasks. When I cook with someone assertive, I'm so relieved that I let them take charge completely, and become rather useless. When I cook with a chef I become anxious and clumsy, expecting them to judge all my self-taught techniques harshly, which they often do. Power swirls around the kitchen.

However, this needn't be the case. When I cook with a good friend it isn't so at all – we decide what we're going to cook beforehand and are quite strict with the division of labour. When we want to comment on the other's cooking, we are in turn gentle ('Do you think you might want to put a bit less garlic in?') and forceful ('Stop with the fucking garlic'). I cannot think of cooking with another person and not think of my friend F–, without whom whatever 'career' I've found in greed would not have come about.

DINNER ITSELF

I am in a state of happy alertness, listening as a dog might for the noise of the gate as it swings open, which will have me out of my chair and to the window. I am jiggling my knee up and down. Though there's music playing, the flat feels very quiet, still, a stage with a set and no actors. I shift, I check my phone, I peek into our bedroom to see what Lo's wearing. I skip back to the kitchen, open a drink, become lost in reverie and jump when the doorbell rings.

Guests' Arrival

Take their coats and bags, then offer a glass of something, even – especially – if they don't drink. Over-chill white wine, unless it's very good, and keep reds at room temperature. If you are serving beer or martinis, keep the glasses in the freezer because everyone finds this very clever. If you're not making a cocktail it is nice to have some variety, and for this beer and red wine are more than enough. After you've dealt with coats and drinks, bring the arrivals to the rest of the guests. Introduce them loudly to everyone if they don't know anyone, but more importantly, introduce them personally to someone you think they'll like.

Late Guests

A dinner party ought to represent the creation of a kind of Utopia. In Utopia you cannot be late, since time is suspended. And so you should invite guests to come 'around eight' or, more sensibly, 'any time after eight', since you certainly can be early to a Utopia and so upset its delicate balance. Most will come around eight thirty in this case, some a little earlier, some later. It hardly matters. But what does matter, what matters intensely, is that you do not plan to eat at a certain time and become upset or anxious. Have snacks and so on to keep hunger away, if it gets to that. If a guest is very late you should begin without them, especially if you have other guests, and put food aside. They will be much happier not to have caused a stir and will come into a house that is glad at their arrival, rather than one that resents them.

Guests Cancelling

Most of the time, cancellations come from something unforeseen or distressing and the canceller will feel rather guilty. Be gracious and tell them that it's OK, that you'll make it happen another time. This is a form of hospitality in itself, extending the kindness of your table to life's complications. If someone cancels too often, simply stop inviting them.

To guard against cancellation becoming a real problem, do not invite so few people that one dropping out will spoil the night; nor should you invite a group so linked to one person that that person's cancellation will have a knock-on effect. *Or* do, and when everyone cancels, rejoice at regaining the evening, now free of stimulation and full of good food.

If you want to invite people to replace missing guests, don't tell them they're a late addition – this can be a bit hurtful. If you're inviting at the last minute, call on the phone – so you get an immediate response. Messages often go unreplied and it's best not to invite multiple people by message at once, in case they all say 'yes' and you're overwhelmed.

Travelling Guests

We take the last train from Totnes to London and find that there are no trains to the airport till six am. A night not-falling-asleep in Polo Bar. Couple opposite have long straight black hair, wear motorcycle leathers, eat stacks of pancakes with ice cream. A train, a shuttle, a plane and finally the bus from Ciampino to Termini show us the sharp Roman sky and winter sun, shining triumphant on the last day of the year. At the house of blue statues and gold rings, the table is heavy with thick glasses and country wine. Lo' sleeps on a pile of clothes and I sit with J– hearing the evening's plan – a dinner, a party, another party – as she feeds me slices of bread and butter, crisps and olives. E– returns from the studio, all arms and legs and mouth, and we go to buy prosecco and confetti, have a cheeky little drink at the tabaccheria, and I do not sleep until next year.

Hospitality is kindness underpinned by a foreknowledge of need. In hot countries, water is offered immediately, while in the wet and dreary British Isles we give hot tea. If someone has come straight from travelling, ask them if they'd like to wash and give them a fresh towel. If dinner isn't for a while, ask if they'd like a snack, or need a coffee, though they might just want a drink. And provide the Wi-Fi password as a matter of course, a trick that solicits great gratitude, like water in a desert.

It is nice to serve travellers a meal that communicates the place they're visiting. By this I don't mean serving shepherd's pie in England or haggis in Scotland, though both can be delicious, but incorporating geography, physical and social, into the food. Local cheeses, meat, wine or beer are beyond fashions and influences. In the countryside it's easiest to express locality through ingredients, while in the city cultural influences are more important. What does an east London suburb mean for food? Manchester? Cornwall? My best memories of eating abroad are coloured by the feeling that I've had something people eat at home that couldn't be found in a restaurant.

> *G– shows us a book of black-and-white photographs of Kyiv – he has the proud nationalism of an emigré. J– is making blinis in the kitchenette with S–. We eat, first, blinis with red caviar – salmon, I think – little almost-horrible fishy balls that explode in the mouth with the warmish blini. This half-disgustingness is important to caviar, a sense of the absurd. Then we have the best borscht I've ever eaten – J–'s recipe, from her grandmother. It has little bits of beef in it, straddles sweet and savoury. We are served, then, pelmeni with beef and pork, very, very good. The night drifts on happily – there is ice cream and stories of life in the nineties: G– beaten by a ticket inspector for skipping his fare; his father – a surgeon – asking criminal associates to beat up some older boys bullying G– and his friends; bumping into thugs on the subway who tell him they're going to 'take him to the forest', so pretending to be deaf, and they befriending him, having to keep up the pretence. Home in a taxi and sleeping well.*

Quiet, Shy Guests and Anxious Hosts

Some people need to be drawn out of themselves. If, after you've introduced them around, they're still struggling to mingle, talk to them yourself and bring others into the conversation. Sit them beside you and be indulgent. And it is a further kindness to give them a simple and unrushed task – peeling potatoes, stoning fruit. They'll feel useful and important rather than anxious, and most often they'll start chatting to you as you cook and, in the breathing space this allows, feel much more able to enter the fray. At nursery I was petrified of the other children and asked to sort pebbles by size. I think of this whenever I give someone peas to pod.

Hosts can be anxious too. A friend of mine, a great host and a wonderful cook, relies heavily on his position in the kitchen to ward off his guests, whom he finds overwhelming. Lo' will often hand-make pasta at the beginning of a dinner, sitting at the table surrounded by her guests, and finds this gives her the time to feel at ease and dip in and out of the conversation. Anxiety shouldn't stop you from hosting, but should be taken seriously. Find a trick that calms your initial nervousness – peel apples, pit olives – and don't worry if your conversation is lax, since your guests will see you're busy and think nothing of it. Enjoy watching until you want to join in. If you're entertaining alone, ask someone whose presence calms you to come before everyone else and host with you.

Drinks

After his first wife, my grandmother, died, my grandfather was very upset and drank Champagne every day for a month. He bought himself a deep-fat fryer: he would make excellent chips with voluminous amounts of Parmesan. It was probably rather distressing for my father, a doctor, but I adored this period, characterised by hours in front of the TV and many small bowls of cheesy chips. After mourning, he remarried, an Anglo-Scot, and moved north of the border to an old manse, which had been a doss house. Memorable, because its simplicity and elegance were more perfect than almost anything I had eaten before, was a lunch of buttered asparagus and very good, fresh fried eggs with a glass of white wine. No recipe is required and the only instruction is that the eggs be the best you can get, and that it helps if your eighty-year-old grandfather has made a trip to his cellar to fetch wine, his daily exercise.

I try to have either wine or beer available. If you can get your guests to drink beer before dinner, you'll save money on wine and will lessen the likelihood of drunkenness. The beer served before dinner should be whichever lager you prefer, commercial or otherwise, as long as it's reasonably light and well chilled. Keep an eye on the table throughout the night, making sure there's always wine and water. The latter is something I'm working on.

If you can and want to spend the money, think about matching the wine with what you're cooking (buttery white with fish, light red with chicken, heavy red with beef and so on – whole forests have perished for books on the subject) but don't be overzealous. The zealous tend to be disguising dullness or a drinking problem. I consider it rather more chic to have house wines – red and white – that you know to be good and you serve with almost anything. Reasonable and inexpensive wine can be bought from most wine merchants, whose cheaper bottles tend to be much better than those of equivalent price in supermarkets.

The best meals I've eaten have been paired with cheap wine – carafes of prosecco in Italy, jugs of *tinto* in Spain, unmarked bottles in France and bottom-shelf stuff in London. While some cheap wines are undeniably bad, others are perfectly fine – cheap, brash reds, especially with meat and pasta. You can find good cheap wine at wine shops, the more old-fashioned the better. In such places, a bumbling man in a pink shirt will be more than happy to tell you how often he drinks the cheaper stuff, and will hopefully point you toward the discounted bin-ends. Modern wine shops, on the other hand, rarely sell anything costing less than three hours of minimum wage, and the people who work in them live in a fantasy world in which this is sustainable. Because of this discrepancy, it's easier to find a good cheap wine in West London, which rings with old money, than among the tower blocks and warehouses of the East. If you're intimidated by wine shops, which are intimidating places, supermarket wines are generally preferable to those sold at off-licences. The former are carefully sourced to be of a reasonable quality, while the wholesalers who supply off-licences have less to lose, knowing they're supplying a customer who values convenience above everything else. Besides, their mark-ups are generally much greater.

My favourite wine shop is Cuckoo Wines in Dalston, which is run by a pair of incredibly friendly brothers, happy to cater to everyone from yummy mummies and account managers to drunks and students. They have the best selection of inexpensive wine in London, and one of the brothers will happily tell you all about each bottle, while the other makes fun of him, claiming he knows much less than he makes out. This is untrue.

There are few fashionable 'natural' wines that go well with food, most being too acidic, although my peers disagree. It's a shame, because traditionally made wine has much subtler flavours and, most importantly, a bottle of quality can be bought for considerably less than one branded as natural. They're generally best before food, as an aperitif.

If you're serving eight people, a good amount to buy is four bottles – two of better quality, two that aren't so good – with the assumption that the third and fourth will likely not be touched, and if touched it will be late, when everyone's already drunk on your nice wine and the wine they've brought. If your guests' appetites are voracious, or if they don't bring any wine, you should suggest they pop to an off-licence, unless you're too far from open shops, in which case it's good to keep extra in stock.

Ask anyone who doesn't drink alcohol what they'd like to drink before they come. The sober are particular, sometimes eccentric, in their choices, and will be incredibly grateful for the question. If they're not forthcoming, buy Diet Coke, non-alcoholic beer and sparkling water.

It's rotten when someone places a cap – or less commonly, because it's harder, the cork – back onto a wine bottle. There are two reasons for this: the first is practical. Most wine will improve, even if slightly, with oxygenation. The fact that this won't be noticeable with a bottle consumed reasonably quickly doesn't matter – what matters is that putting the cap back on shows you don't know this. The second is much more important. If you put the cap back onto a bottle, it signals to all but the bravest guest that they may not refill their glass, that you are staking a claim of ownership. It is, quite simply, ungenerous.

Giving short and light descriptions of a drink can be charming, a nice ritual, if the mood is right. But arrogantly going into terroir, nose, vineyard, vintage and so on is vulgar, and as boring as trainspotting with worse politics.

I am now sober but wasn't when I began writing this book, and think it would be remiss to miss a note on the martini, which I still love making. They are dangerous beasts, so I'm watchful of how many are drunk. I tend to offer only one and, if asked, will make another. But I'll make excuses after that, for the third martini spells ruin for most. The same goes for all spirits. Drunks at the table are utterly boring, repeating conversations and getting into arguments. As a host, you should have a vague idea of what your guests have consumed, and, though it is imperative you keep people's glasses topped up, it's also sensible to subtly withdraw service from anyone who's had too much. Sure, the dream is only inviting those who can handle their drink, but such a rule would preclude half my friends.

My Martini

Pour a jot of vermouth into a glass and swirl it around, then discard. If I am making more than one, I'll pour this vermouth into the next glass, if not I'll usually pour it back into the bottle. The slope of a martini glass is important here – providing the right traction to take on enough vermouth. Now place a handful of ice in each glass and set them aside. You can skip this step if they've come from the freezer. Fill a shaker with lots of ice and a glass of gin (or vodka, I suppose) kept at room temperature and shake, rapidly, for thirty or so seconds. The shaker will be cold. Strain into the glass (after removing the ice cooling it), top with an olive and the desired amount of brine.

When to Eat

I tend to serve up about an hour after my guests have arrived as this gives everyone time to relax, get to know one another and the space they're in. It also means that you don't need to have finished doing everything before they arrive. Though remember that there's absolutely nothing wrong with cooking when your guests are there, simply that you may find your attention split.

Do not to be fixed with eating times. Check if guests need to eat earlier – they might have children, a disability, be busy – and be ever-ready to make adjustments.

Against Plating Up

Though it seems normal now, dining à la Russe, in courses with food pre-plated, is a culinary invention imported from aristocratic Russia. Having plated courses relied on a large number of servants and indentured people, which the cruel conditions of that country ensured. Because of this, rather than a plethora of dishes to be taken onto a plate, each became distinct. This translated well to restaurants, which began to be established in the late eighteenth century as a way for the new rich to pool resources and experience aristocratic forms of dining.

Eating à la Russe is fun – having a dish prepared, curated, weighed and balanced by a team of cooks and placed before you like art is exciting. There is something democratic about an inexpensive restaurant – in Italy, say – where the pooling of resources makes it possible for chefs, waiters and cleaners to sit and order like a prince.

But this requires a well-organised team to work smoothly and has no place in the home. And so I almost never plate up – it seems oddly formal, and causes the host unnecessary work, creating an awkward pause while you mess about with presentation, leaving the food on the first plate to go cold. Instead, serve food family-style.

Pappardelle alla Danielle

Eight of us were crammed into our tiny kitchen, the leaves of the table extended, with no space for anyone but me to stand. I was slow cooking a cabbage I planned to serve alongside pappardelle with truffle, but someone suggested mixing the two, producing a perfect unity of the earth's humblest and most respected offspring.

SERVES 8

100g butter, plus a knob for the cabbage
A glug of olive oil
1 head of Savoy cabbage, finely chopped
½ a bottle of white wine
Sea salt
2 handfuls of finely grated Parmesan (plus the rinds, if you have them)
2 x 50g jars of truffle sauce
500g dried pappardelle

---

1. In a large pan, melt the knob of butter with the oil and add the cabbage. Toss a little, but don't worry about coating all of it – you won't be able to.
2. Add the white wine and a generous pinch of salt. If you have Parmesan rinds, add these too.
3. Cook, covered, over a low heat for 2 hours, stirring occasionally, until very tender and buttery. Add more wine if the cabbage is drying out.

4. In a large pan, melt the remaining butter with two small jars of truffle sauce – the ratio is one jar to 250g of pasta – and allow 10 or so minutes for the truffle to properly infuse into the butter.
5. Cook the pasta in salted boiling water until al dente and toss in the sauce. Throw in the two handfuls of finely grated Parmesan and mix it all with the cabbage.

Family Style

It's a funny term, one I only learnt on holiday with a lot of Americans, who'd describe any large platter of meat or pasta in a restaurant as 'family style'. I rather liked this way of describing something I'd never thought to describe, since it was so normal to me, which conferred a closeness on the diners.

There are two ways of serving family style – from the vessels you've cooked in or on serving ware. It's easier, and perhaps less fussy, to do the former. And there's a lot that's grand about a big, battered saucepan containing pasta, while anything cooked in a casserole or clay pot ought to stay in it.

But be careful about serving food in pots and pans, and be guided by a general rule: if the vessel dwarfs the food – as a saucepan will dwarf peas – or leaves it looking sparse – as a roasting dish does potatoes – it's better to serve the food on something smaller. If you don't have serving dishes, use plates or bowls. This is especially true of sauces – from gravy to fresh mayonnaise – which look much better as small lakes than large puddles. Soup, on the other hand, should be served in its pan and never a tureen, which crosses the border into fussiness.

For roast meats, a platter is almost a necessity, since meat should be given its ceremonial due. A bird should go in the centre and will look beautiful with its potato and vegetable accompanying it. Equally, a stew served on a bed of polenta is quite a sight, as is a fish atop samphire. Such grand platters unclutter the table and inspire focus. Singularly beautiful foods – artichokes or rare beef, for instance – benefit from having their own platter, so that the brightness of their looks is not dimmed.

Toasting

The act of being thankful for food and company should not be left to the religious alone. If a meal can begin with a few words of gratitude, humble and kind, it will be enriched. But the register of grace – the religious connotations it holds and the somewhat sombre mood it creates – can be amiss at dinner.

A toast does the same in an exuberant register. Its only rule is that you must ensure everyone's glasses are full, which you can do as an introduction to the toast itself – 'Charge your glasses!' The first toast of a meal can simply be to thank your guests for coming. It can blossom into thanking those who've worked to produce the food you're eating, the farmers and labourers, cheesemakers and butchers, and can movingly include absent friends.

If someone has recently died, the small hush a toast to them will bring is cathartic, while the toast's essence as a celebration will have them remembered within life's joys as well as its silences.

Stock toasts can say all this in one: the British *cheers,* the Ukrainian *budmo*, the Polish *na zdrowie*, with its Slavic equivalents, and the French *salut*, with its Romance equivalents. My mother would often say 'To the idiots!' which is taken from the Armenian mystic Gurdjieff, a remark on the absurdity of our individuality. After a toast, you should try to touch everyone's glasses and meet their eyes. Clinking glasses may be impossible, but making eye contact never is. Like a kiss, a hug or a handshake, it is a firm recognition of another's presence.

If you'd like to add a little more ritual, you might toast like the Spanish and place your glass firmly down after it has touched others, before you take a sip, which ensures you'll have sex. To add humour to this ritual, you may rub your glass's base clockwise, ensuring orgasm. '*Quien no apoya no folla, y quién no recorre no se corre.*'

Speeches

It had become cold outside, the damp cold of summer night in the English countryside, and the frogs had begun to hop into the kitchen through the open door. Lo' picked one up and showed it to the table, met with squeals of delight and murmurs of interest. I brought the cake over, covered with whipped cream and sugared sage leaves, and as I began to cut it I felt overcome with happiness, looking at friends from so many places, with those they loved and were able to love. I stood again and said, 'I want to praise modernity. I want to say I would never have lived at any other time. I can't help but remember that the ease with which we are here, the ease with which we can love one another, has never before existed.' I continued such platitudes, words met first with giggling to puncture my self-seriousness, and after, noises of agreement.

I have never given a speech I regret, nor thought someone else's a mistake or out of place. But almost every speech I've thought to give and haven't has lingered on my mind as a failure to rise to the occasion. I am thinking most of those easy, impromptu speeches at the beginning of dinner or at its end, when the genius of kindness flows from one's mouth. Of course, I am gregarious and sentimental, verging on mawkish, and would think this.

A toast is not always enough and speeches lend a ritualised backing to sentiments that might not otherwise be expressed, to so many or so simply. If you can, you should stand for a speech, since this pulls the table toward you and gives your words the weight and comedy they'll need. A speech should be given at a birthday, or to acknowledge a celebration even if it is not the meal's primary focus. It should not be delivered to a table fewer than six, or be too long: a sentence about the celebrated, another about the evening and a joke. And, since a speech's worth is in its intention, you needn't worry too much about the words themselves. Sometimes a speech will lead to others, and the meal will be punctuated by praise and jollity.

Snacks

Snacks should correspond to what you're serving for dinner – light before heavy and something more substantial before something light. Their purpose is not to sate the appetite but to excite it.

Oysters are my favourite thing to have before a meal – they cause a great deal of excitement, even for those who refuse to eat them. Nothing is more beautiful or speaks so eloquently of luxury than oysters nestled on a plate of ice, and knowing how to open one marks out a good host. And best of all they're not terribly expensive, since no one expects more than one each. Serving very cold bottles of Guinness with your oysters is a considered choice as well as an exercise in frugality.

There's a reason the Italians, who like to snack so much before dinner that they've invented a whole, fourth, snacking meal, love crisps: the salt makes you thirsty and their ephemeral nature means they won't fill you up. Olives, too, by verging on the unpleasant, stimulate and excite the mouth. Very good-quality fresh vegetables, cut into batons, are wonderful just with a little salt. Here you'll see the difference between a young organic carrot, sweet and complex, and a large watery one from the supermarket. A poached artichoke is very classy. It's nice to borrow from the Iranians and place nuts and herbs on the table: the fragrance flirts with your guests' senses, and there are few pleasures as surprising as a single mint leaf.

I generally don't serve bread and cheese as a snack before dinner because it's too filling, and I'll never stop thinking the habit in English restaurants of bringing bread and butter to the table to be eaten before anything else has arrived is odd, since bread should be eaten alongside everything else.

If dinner's going to be very light, cured meats and cheeses are a good addition, but make sure not to put too much on the table, since we are only animals and will find them hard to resist, our stomachs never quite believing there will be food tomorrow.

Against Starters

I never serve anything elaborate as a starter for a dinner party, and rarely serve anything self-contained at all. There will be snacks, but they will never need real prep, be cooked just before they're eaten, or require massed attention.

This is a rule of expedience, yes, but also of style. Serving starters isn't a relaxed business, since they require the host to rise from the table after they've been eaten and return to the kitchen, carrying away the dirty plates, causing a rupture in the conversation, forcing dinner to pause and begin again.

However, if you have something special – a particularly good fresh fruit or vegetable, a pâté from far away, a sausage from your home – and you want to make sure it isn't lost as a snack or within the meal, it's nice to have it before the other dishes. I was terribly touched to have two spears of my host's first asparagus with a dash of butter, touched too to be given a third of a peach from one of three a new tree had produced. Such gestures spell magic – such magic does not require a change of plates.

Mains

When we returned the house smelt delicious, lamb was cooking. The hot water was not working so I warmed myself with tea, and sat on a sofa reading. Lyons, the Irish brand – the brand the M—s drink – is one of my favourite teas: bitter and deep. Later, we had a leg of lamb from a farm not five miles away. Beside it were – all from the garden – lightly buttered kohlrabi with mustard seeds, beans that spoke of summer though it was not to be seen outside, excellent potatoes crisped in the beast's fat and small summer leeks cooked, again, in butter. I had three helpings, washed down with many glasses of cider from an uncle's farm.

When you're planning what you'll cook for dinner, keep the rule of simplicity in your mind. A simple menu lets your guests taste and appreciate each thing you serve, is less work and is far better to look at.

I think of the main course like this: the central dish, its supporters and the sauce. If I am roasting an animal or serving a stew, I'll cook two to four things to go with it – a chicken with blanched cabbage, buttered carrots, roast potatoes and gravy, or beef and plums with polenta and chard. If I'm making something more self-contained, like pasta, I'll put salad on the table. The diners will not be overwhelmed by an excess of flavours, some clashing, but will find their plates unified.

Such simple plates greatly decrease the chance of making a mistake or feeling overwhelmed, and seem entirely intuitive. Yet I had to do a certain amount of unlearning to practise such simplicity. I blame recipe books, which – because doing so is boring – don't include the simple preparations for vegetables one should serve beside meat, but provide recipes that take as much time and thought as any central dish. So much work fills the potential host with trepidation and overwhelms them when they come to cook. Yotam Ottolenghi, the most influential cookbook writer in twenty-first-century England, has a lot to answer for here, though the sheer weight of the good he's brought to our tables far outweighs this small gripe.

It's helpful to have central dishes in your arsenal that you can trot out without stress or worry. The recipes at the end of this book are from my own repertoire. And, importantly, cooking food you are familiar with is not just easier but allows for experimentation and personalisation in a way that following a recipe cannot. When you can cook an array of things well, when you come to understand them, you begin to understand cooking's principles and start to be able to create other dishes entirely from scratch.

Desserts

I did not grow up in a dessert-centric household and so remember when we had dessert – almost all on Sundays, after lunch. This would be a crumble in winter or strawberries and cream in summer. I remember disappointment, because my father cooked with little sugar and we weren't allowed to add it to our strawberries, though I'm sure this was a good thing for my palate. Otherwise, there'd be desserts on holidays, the normal stuff at Christmas and Easter – heavy fruitcakes or puddings set afire. I was scandalised by people who had dessert every night. I still am.

When we first started having people to dinner we didn't often make dessert; it often didn't occur to me. Lo' saw the error and began to make cakes, pastries, panna cotta, flavouring and infusing and constructing, her artist's mind afire in sweets. But, as with all good artists, she became bored and stopped making desserts. I took over.

I am not a brilliant dessert cook, so I've stuck to a pretty simple dessert menu: two cakes, one a sort of sponge that can incorporate any fruit, which I serve with custard, the other a chocolate cake I infuse with herbs. If I don't have time to make a cake, I'll poach fruit to serve with custard. If I want to be especially English, I'll make sticky toffee pudding and, on special occasions, a trifle.

Again, the rule of simplicity has given me a selection of dishes I can make with great ease, and within whose perimeters I can experiment. If I was more inclined toward desserts the list would be longer, just as my main courses would be fewer if I cared less for the savoury.

Desserts should be served a little while – half an hour to an hour – after dinner, to give time for digestion and to keep your guests at the table. They should be placed in the centre of the table and eaten off little plates with little spoons. Second helpings should be encouraged. They are most important for people who don't drink, since they'll have consumed much less sugar than anyone who does.

Cheese

I believe that the tradition of having cheese *after* rather than *before* dinner represents the leftovers of a charming kind of frugality – cheese, gram for gram, is more expensive than almost any other food. If served before the meal it disappears quickly, costs a lot and ruins appetites.

If the meal has been good and your guests are not very greedy, the cheese will not be demolished, and most will have a slice or two. They will also think you are grown up and sophisticated. I do not think large, varied cheeseboards are necessary and will usually only serve three cheeses at a maximum – a blue cheese, a hard cheese and a soft cheese – but more often I only serve one or two.

My preference is for cheese from somewhere close – if, for instance, you're in the English West Country, you will have access to a large variety of local cheeses, which are generally easy to find since most towns will have a cheesemonger. As London, in my mind at least, exists in a temporal realm divorced from its geography, it is permissible to eat cheese from anywhere here, as is the case in any large city.

I don't think expensive crackers deserve much respect. It is best to stick with Scots oatcakes (Nairn's are the best) or water biscuits (Carr's) and, for those given over to excess, digestive biscuits for blue cheese, though I have never seen the need. It's nice to have a bunch of grapes, a pear or some good apples on the board.

A Fruit Bowl

In the eighteenth century, middle-class families, eager to impress newfound wealth on their guests, would rent fruit for their fruit bowl. The most prized was the pineapple – the British love for this fruit's form is evident in the Dunmore Pineapple, a pineapple-shaped folly in Scotland, where one could never be grown. They would also rent hothouse peaches and apricots, pears, oranges and so on, so that they could bring a laden fruit bowl to the table after dessert, looking like a Dutch still life. Though frugal hosts would abstain, they would never tell their guests to leave off and a greedy-guts might grab a peach to bury their face in. When the fruit was returned the next day, the fruitier would charge a flat fee and extra for each piece missing. In small towns one could do a round of dinner parties and see the same fruit in a different house each day.

Bring fruit to the table after dinner. I'd usually bring chocolate too – along with coffee – and I like it after a grand affair, especially if the fruit bowl is prettily adorned. There is good ceremony in a large carved fruit being placed in the centre of the table and greedily eaten. At my table, I like to lean back in my chair and cut slices of apple and pear with a Catalan knife, passing them to whoever's on my left and right. When it's hot I keep fresh fruit in the fridge, which elevates it.

Coffee or Tea

A Polish friend said 'So European!' when I brought the coffee pot to the table after dinner. This is really how philistine the British are seen to be. Offering tea or coffee after dinner is a barometer for the night's mood – if coffee is rejected, your guests probably want to go home. If it is accepted with gusto, they want to stay. If you want them to stay, consider bringing whiskey, amaro or another after-dinner drink along with the pot. If you don't, bring the coffee alone and no alcohol. A guest might request more to drink and, if they do, see to their wishes, but this generally won't happen since most people understand coffee's ritual significance.

Games

We were staying in a house in France and had the two other English people in the village to dinner one night – they had helped us out when we'd first arrived, wineless, to a dark house. The man we knew: funny, nervy, in his early seventies, toothbrush moustache, ever ready with a little joke. His wife we hadn't met and so were disappointed that, when she arrived, her hair dyed jet black and diamonds on her fingers, wrists and ears, she asked if she might have a glass of Coke. We had none, apologised, and so she had white wine. As the evening progressed it became apparent that the Coke was a stalling tactic, for this lady drank, as did her husband. An hour or so into the meal my head whipped round to the sound of metal against glass – a speech? She was knocking her knife against her empty wine glass and, when she had our attention, declared 'There's a problem here!' The drinking continued, flooring two of our party, who made excuses and wobbled up to bed, the second bottle of dessert wine now dead, the white port almost gone. I jumped up and made coffee, strong, and brought it to the table, filling a large cup for each of our elder drunks. 'Port's out', said the woman, her glass newly empty. To this I lied, saying the house was now dry. The coffee seemed to have a reviving effect and the man said 'I suppose we ought to go home', though when he tried to stand up his legs, very thin, wobbled so much that he sat back down. It was necessary for me and the other conscious resident to walk them home, pretending to the man that we needed his help to walk and acting the gallant chaperone to the woman. On the slope to her front door she slipped, falling so quickly that I was pulled with her. 'You fell over! You fell over and pulled me with you!' she said angrily. The next day I went to check on them and to collect some potatoes we'd been promised, and found her up and about, surrounded by books and dust. I was glad, as I'd half thought I might find them dead.

Games after dinner can whip up a havoc of laughter. The fewer rules, the better, and for true joy they must be silly. The first two were made up with our friends Laurie, Abigail and Helena, the last is from the 1920s, and require nothing but sharp wits. The final two games are played with cards. Every house should possess a deck of cards: they are cheap and take up little space.

Find the glasses – a simple game to be played with someone's spectacles, the thinner and less visible the better. Everyone, save the hider, closes their eyes while the hider places the glasses somewhere odd in the room. I don't know why such a simple game is made so much funnier by the object being glasses, but it is.

Categories – a game almost without rules, when one must say things of a certain category one after the other in turn, going around the table. The categories can include, but are not limited to, clothes, kitchen utensils and condiments. The duller the category, the better the game.

Poor pussy – a parlour game. One guest must kneel before another, their eyes wide and simpering, occasionally mewling and meowing, pretending to be a forlorn cat. The standing guest must look down, stroke their hair and declare 'Poor pussy'. The player who gets the most 'poor pussies' before laughing wins.

President – a game for three or more, but best for eight players with two packs of cards. For the first round, the cards are dealt clockwise by the host to every player, until no more are left. The player to the host's right may now lay down multiple cards of the same rank (for instance two threes, three clubs or six aces if two packs are being used) and the next player must lay down the same number, or more, of cards of the same or a higher rank (for instance, upon two threes must be laid at least two fours, though any higher number or rank of cards is permitted, for instance, four eights.)

If the same rank is played, the next player is skipped, unless they too have the same rank. In this case, the player beside them is skipped. If someone cannot play cards of the same or a higher rank, they may skip and will shed no cards. Play continues until all but the last player have shed their cards.

The first player to shed all their cards becomes the president and the last player with cards becomes the shithead. In a game of six or more, the second player to shed their cards becomes the vice president, and the second to last player becomes the vice shithead. Those in the middle are the bourgeoisie, proud to exploit no one, but never extending a helping hand.

The shithead must give their best two cards to the president, who may give the shithead whichever two cards they please, the same pattern is true for the vices, though they only swap one card. The shithead and vice shithead must behave in a snivelling and deferential manner to those at the table, while the president and vice president should be haughty. All players should heap scorn upon the shitheads, laughing when they lose, hissing when they win. The president deals and goes first.

In President the highest ranked card is the two, followed by the ace, then the king, et cetera, and the lowest is three. Jokers are wild cards and may be placed in the stead of any other.

Bullshit – a game that is best with a large group and many packs, though it can be played with three. The host deals all the cards clockwise, save the last, which they place in the middle, face up. The person to their right plays first, laying a card, or many, face down in the middle, declaring the number of cards and worth, which must be higher than the previous card, for instance three fours on top of a three. However, this can be a lie, since no one else can see the cards. If another player believes this to be the case they must shout 'bullshit' *before* the next card is played. If the player has lied, they must pick up all the cards, but if they have been accused in error, the accuser must pick everything up. The winner is the first to get rid of all their cards.

In Bullshit, the ace is low and the king is high.

Getting People to Leave

It is the good host's dilemma: a dinner party no-one wants to leave. But you are tired, have begun to fade, have begun to loathe your guests. Guests who you know very well can be told straight, but the rest, those manners prevent you from simply throwing out – how do you get rid of them?

Well, if everyone's drinking the best thing is to stop serving alcohol. This pulls at the heartstrings because it goes against the host's imperative, to provide. I begin subtly – all evening I will have been keeping an eye on the table, making sure there's always wine within reach. I'll stop doing this and let the table dry out. Guests will look at their glasses, check the empty bottles and I'll avert my eyes. Perhaps one will ask if there's any wine and I'll say we've run out, even if I know there's more. For this reason I store drinks out of immediate sight, lest someone spies one. As the table dries I will begin yawning, openly, exaggeratedly. If anyone says anything to me I'll blink my eyes as if returning to consciousness. This is enough if your guests are reasonably sober, but drunk guests ignore cues. At this point I'll offer herbal tea – nothing kills a mood more quickly, and few refuse to take the point, though those who would might say they can go to the shop. It is at this point that one must abandon all decorum and explain that you want to go to bed.

Cleaning Up

Put everything on the side, let your guests help carry things if they want, but don't expect them to, and discourage them if they're drunk.

The one rule of cleaning up is that you don't let your guests help. My mother says this: 'It's my kitchen, and I know where everything goes. Besides, if you suggest I help wash up in your house, I'll walk out.' You can let them clear the table – and think people who do are helpful – but no more, because nothing kills the mood faster than everyone getting up to clean. Well, aside from one thing: when the host leaves the table to start washing up while everyone is still seated, leaving the guests uncomfortable, thinking they ought to leave.

A trope I love, have loved since I was a kid, is the assessment given of a dinner after the guests have left by the hosts as they clean, wash up, have a final glass of something or make tea. It is what gets me through awful dinner parties with brash, crude people – knowing I'll soon be alone with someone I love and respect when everyone has left. If you're entertaining alone, invite a close friend who'll stay for a little while after everyone has gone, with whom you can gossip and whose presence will soften the shock of a suddenly silent house.

As for cleaning up itself – if you have the energy to do it, it'll make your life easier. I've never owned a dishwasher – because of renting odd apartments, and also because almost nothing I own is dishwasher safe – but if I did I would load it. Otherwise, don't fret – there is meditation in cleaning up. To spare myself the full weight of the dinner's mess I am quite fastidious about cleaning as I cook, otherwise dirty things pile on other dirty things and become overwhelming.

Moreover, you should clean as much as you can before your guests arrive. This isn't about pride – there's nothing wrong with a sink full of dirty spoons and pans or sideboards covered in flour. It's for you. Waking up and finding all the plates and glasses on top of those spoons and pans, and that spilled water has turned the flour on the sides to glue, is too much to bear, especially if you're hungover. You will resent yesterday's revelling and forget the fun you had. Before dinner, on the other hand, you'll be spritely and awake, excited for the evening ahead, and cleaning will breeze past.

RECIPES

Then me and M– walk into C – a nice walk: shady, on a dirt road, and only a little over ten minutes. We buy sausages, potatoes, wine and eggs from two shops – one is the butcher and the other has cured meat, and is darker and dustier, but has better fruit and vegetables. Though this is not saying much as neither are good. I insist that there must be more shops, but our bags are heavy and we don't really look. We want, too, to get home and begin drinking. The house has one hectare and many tables in different, strategic places. We settle onto a little round table and watch the sun dim, talking airily, happily, sleepily, drinking wine, eating olives. At about ten we are a little hungry and want something warm, so I boil potatoes, fry sausages, flash-fry courgettes and make a tomato salad. I finish the potatoes in oil so they are a little crispy, with plenty of rosemary from the hills. There is a slight chill in the air and I curse myself for leaving my autumn suit in Barcelona. The mystery of the bad vegetables is solved on our last day when, walking to the station, we pass the overabundant weekly market in the town square.

Notes on Ingredients and Method

All recipes are for six to eight people, unless otherwise specified.

Money and quality – Some things are worth spending money on: meat, honey, cream, fruit, dried pulses, tinned tomatoes. Some things aren't: potatoes, cooking wine, sugar, flour, vinegar, frozen peas, cabbages.

The point is not an exhaustive list but to be indicative. There is a fetishisation of price in food culture – it's always been there – but I think the idea that because something is expensive it's good is becoming more pronounced. The best explanation I've heard for this is that since young professionals cannot, in many places, afford the big things their parents could, they must assert their class in other ways. Olives and sour wine from a shop with 'Provisionals' or 'Victuals' in its name have replaced mortgages and new cars. 'We would never have eaten out so often' say parents, accidental millionaires who had their own kitchens by their mid-twenties.

A general rule against this is: if you're going to cook something with other things, or with spices, it needn't be of the best quality, while if you are going to serve something with little intervention, you need the best you can get. Butter to fry should be the cheapest, while butter for bread should be the best; eggs for baking and eggs for eating alone follow the same rule, as do olive oils and salt.

You should never talk about the expense of an ingredient with reverence, only mockingly. You can talk about its rarity, seasonal or otherwise, the difficulties of finding it, or its specialness to you, because all these things will make your guests feel lucky. But to talk of something's cost is simply to inspire guilt in those you are feeding, and is vulgar besides.

Seasonality – Fresh food tends to taste better and be cheaper while in season, and gives a grammar to the culinary calendar, providing excitement and relief with each new month.

Locality – There are two types of local food: that which is made near you and that which reflects the tastes of the people you live amongst. Do not focus so much on the first that you miss all the second has to offer.

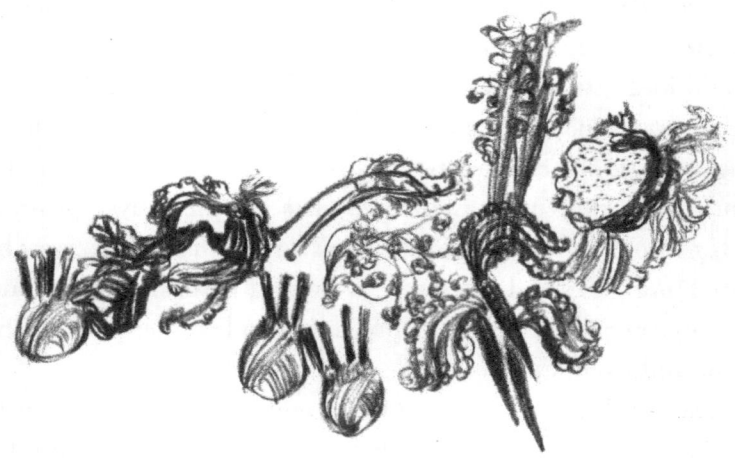

Organic, artisan, low-carbon – Yes, they often taste better and, yes, they may contribute less to environmental destruction, big business and climate change, but they are also more expensive. Such expense puts them out of the reach of many people and divorces buying them from any moral good. Do not feel guilty if you can't afford to shop 'ethically', and do not feel moral if you can. If you care, join campaigns, sign petitions, write letters and protest. It is the overhaul of our wasteful food systems, rather than a single shop or farm, that will make a difference.

> *The entrance to Tbilisi's biggest market is dusty, and the market is made of ramshackle structures, its floor is of dirt, the tables are plain. In fact, the first part – selling fruit – is uncovered and made, simply, of a rectangle of tables – stallholders inside, fruit on the outside. There are piles of tangerines, selling for one lari a pound – twenty-five pence. Five or six varieties of grapes, heaped up, light pink to deep purple, and my favourite, which are almost translucent, like coloured glass. Beetroots are arranged beautifully, their tails facing the sky. There are tiny, almost circular cucumbers, many different peppers. Often vegetables, especially peppers, are packed into large plastic sacks, sometimes see-through, so that they stand by themselves, giving a grand feeling of plenty. Behind the herb stalls are gigantic plastic bags of herbs: dill, parsley and coriander. The fresh haricot and kidney beans are beautiful too, sold in large flat trays, deep purple and pink, all three, four and five lari a pound. Pasta is sold from large paper sacks – macaroni, penne, soup pastas, spaghetti. And then there is fruit leather, hung up as if on a washing line, in deep reds, greens, purples and browns, costing one lari a sheet. G– says that most of the workers here are Azeri and that this is also the case for people who toil the land. I wish I had recorded every price, but we were so laden with bags, and I was so tired, that such sensible things were beyond me. My shopping list, too, I deleted from my phone – deleting objects as I bought them. But from memory I bought four cauliflowers, many bunches of grapes, two bottles – five-hundred millilitres – of Kakhetian sunflower oil (three lari each), one kilo of pears, one kilo of green tomatoes (two and a half*

lari per kilo), two kilos of beautiful, misshapen tomatoes (four lari per kilo), fresh haricot beans, shelled – so bright and of many colours, like jelly beans (four lari per kilo), two kilos of broad beans, half yellow and half mottled; parsley, dill, tarragon, the latter out of season so harder to find; gigantic bunches of beetroot leaves with tiny baby beetroots attached to the roots; walnuts. Everything is very cheap, save walnuts, which are almost as much as they would be from Lidl in the UK.

Measurements for savoury food – I have kept measurements free and vague for four reasons. The first is practical – when I record my recipes, I don't record exact amounts save where I've used a whole tin or packet, since I cook with instinct rather than a scale. The second is somewhat philosophical, somewhat practical – ingredients differ greatly, one chicken is unlike another, and a cook must learn to appreciate this. And the third pedagogical – a certain vagueness forces each cook to impose themselves on a recipe: they must decide what they feel generosity is in regard to butter, or the way one roughly and distractedly chops an onion. The fourth lies in my own shortcomings. There are many wonderful books and blogs for inexperienced cooks, without which I – untrained and without national food culture – would be scarcely able to cook an egg. I doubt I could write such recipes, and so hope my reader will have a reasonable knowledge of cooking and a willingness to forgive my poetic – culinary – licence.

Tinned tomatoes – I once heard that whole tinned tomatoes are better than those already chopped and have stuck to this notion religiously. If I don't want to cook them whole, I blend them, and if there's no blender to hand, use a fork to mash them. Expensive tinned tomatoes are worth the expense, sadly, though I can't notice the difference between the best in the supermarket and anything pricier.

Oil – I have two olive oils in my kitchen: a light oil, which needn't be virgin but has a higher burn point, for cooking; and a high-quality virgin oil for salads. Alongside these are sunflower oil, which I use for deep frying, and sesame oil, which I use in dressings.

Garlic – Not all garlic is the same: for instance, European garlic has a stronger flavour than Chinese garlic. Generally, the better the garlic, the stronger its taste.

Sausages – The recipes in this book require high meat content (eighty per cent plus) sausages. This isn't to disparage any others: I really like the cheap, bready sausages serve in greasy spoons and wish a company would start making one with high-welfare pork. But such sausages cannot make a ragu.

Cooking wine – It is a fallacy that wine for cooking should be good enough to drink. If anything, using drinking wine for cooking is an insult to the prowess of the vineyard. Aside from very cheap wines enhanced with sugar – not really wines at all – all wine is created equal where cooking is concerned. I certainly have never been able to tell the difference.

Stock – Making stock from leftover vegetables, bones and so on is good, but hard work and it takes up a lot of space in the freezer. If this isn't an option for you, the various jelly 'stock pots' are pretty good. To elevate them before use, make them up to the packet's proportions and boil with a carrot, half an onion and two garlic cloves, alongside any other stock vegetables, spices or herbs you desire, for half an hour.

Beans – To my dismay, I have found that higher-quality, and more expensive, beans are worth it, whether tinned, jarred or dried.

Garnishes – Dishes can be lifted by a garnish of herbs or spices, but only if it's honest: a garnish, a twig of rosemary for instance, that does not appear in the dish's preparation is a lie. This differs, of course, from the addition of large amounts of herbs – a handful of parsley over pasta – since their purpose is flavour rather than decoration and signal.

Pasta Sauces

Slutty Spaghetti

Easy and cheap, this is an excellent recipe to make for a large group, perfect for an impromptu weekday meal.

I made this pasta the day my sister left Barcelona, because she wanted something filling and comforting for the plane. She calls it 'slutty pasta', which is a derivation of pasta puttanesca, though this is actually more like a spaghetti alla norma because of the aubergine. But adding the aubergine is up to you. I love naming like this, the changing and softening and personalising over time. Other people call it 'slut sauce', 'pasta puttana', 'whore's spaghetti', and make it differently. I would happily serve a large platter of this Anglo-Italian pasta to any group of guests.

2 large aubergines, sort of cubed
A generous glug of olive oil
3 cloves of garlic, peeled and crushed
A pinch of chilli flakes
3 x 400g tins of whole tomatoes, blitzed
A splash of red wine
600g spaghetti
Sea salt
Freshly grated Parmesan, to serve

---

1. Fry the aubergine cubes in olive oil in a large pan until they're golden on each side and soft in the middle, about 10 minutes over a medium heat, and put aside on a plate lined with a sheet of kitchen paper.

2. Now turn the heat down low, let the pan cool a bit and add the garlic and chilli flakes. Fry until golden, adding more oil if necessary.
3. Add the tomatoes to the pan with the garlic and chilli.
4. Bring to the boil, then simmer over a medium heat, stirring every now and then and loosening up with a little red wine, till you've got a rich, tangy sauce, thick, almost jammy. Add the aubergines and stir.
5. Cook your spaghetti in salty boiling water – I haven't told you to season the sauce, that's intentional – and when al dente use tongs or whatever to transfer the pasta to the saucepan. The pasta water that comes with the pasta as you lift it in will season and reinvigorate the sauce. Add a splash more if necessary.
6. This is good served with Parmesan.

Sausage Ragu

This recipe benefits from time, so if I were to serve it on a day I was working, I would prepare it the day before. Otherwise, it is perfect for a Saturday or Sunday.

A recipe borrowing from Marcella Hazan's ragu bolognese, which revolutionised my ideas about ragu entirely, reminding me that it can be a soft, subtle sauce – white save for the light brown of the beef and the pink of the tomato. But not too much tomato and no red wine: white wine, milk, butter. A northern Italian recipe.

1 carrot
2 sticks of celery
2 medium onions, peeled
Olive oil
A knob of butter
Filling of 6 decent-sized, high-meat-content pork sausages
200ml whole milk (or semi-skimmed milk with a little cream)
A generous grating of nutmeg
A generous grinding of black pepper
Sea salt
A glug of dry white vermouth
1 x 400g tin of whole tomatoes, blitzed
600g wholemeal tagliatelle
Freshly grated Parmesan, to serve

1. Make a fine soffrito by finely dicing the carrot, celery and onions, then fry in a large saucepan in olive oil and a knob of butter until the onions are translucent.
2. Add the sausage meat, broken up into little lumps, and fry until browned.
3. Add the milk (and cream, if using) along with the nutmeg, pepper and a little salt and simmer until the milk has reduced.
4. Add the white vermouth and reduce, then add the tomatoes. Bring briefly to the boil, then turn down the heat to the gentlest of simmers, stirring every now and then and adding a little water if necessary, for 3 hours. By that time the sauce should be sweet and light, and a little under-salted.
5. Cook the tagliatelle until al dente in salted boiling water and add to the ragu using tongs, which gets the perfect amount of pasta water into the sauce, giving it its final unctuousness.
6. Serve with Parmesan and pepper.

Soups and Stews

Feather and Stalk Soup

The feathers or fronds of a fennel bulb are a treat and, tragically, are generally removed and discarded before it is sold, almost only to be found at farmer's markets. They have a light anise taste and smell delicious. This soup is a way of harvesting their magic and using everything up, and should be eaten on a wet Tuesday.

1 large onion, peeled
Olive oil
Stalks and feathers of 2 fennel bulbs
2 cloves of garlic, peeled and roughly chopped
1 large potato, peeled
Vegetable stock
Sea salt

---

1. Chop the onion roughly and fry in a generous glug of olive oil in a large saucepan until it is nearly translucent.
2. Quite finely chop the feathers of the fennel, but leave the stalks as large as you can; you will fish them out of the soup before serving. Add to the onion, along with the roughly chopped garlic. Stir and coat with oil and sauté until the fennel has wilted.
3. Chop the potato into small cubes and mix into the pan, then add enough vegetable stock to cover plus an inch, along with two teaspoons of salt if your stock is unsalted. Bring to the boil then reduce the heat and simmer for an hour.
4. Remove the fennel stalks with tongs – though I have tried very

powerful blenders, their fibrous nature seems impossible to escape – and add salt to taste. Blend until smooth, after removing the fennel stalks. Serve the soup. It will be lightly anise flavoured, the feathers dotting the murky broth.

Roast Leek and Potato Soup

My mother would cook two things when I was a child – along with all my unnamed childhood meals – leek and potato soup and British spaghetti bolognese. The soup she'd serve with buttered sliced white bread, which I liked as much as cake. Since I can't remember the house ever having sliced bread in it, my parents having converted from it in the late nineties, such a meal must have been an early staple. This 'elevation' is a nod to her and the nourishment she provided, day in and day out. The roasted leeks give an undertone not dissimilar to truffles.

2 large leeks
Olive oil
Sea salt
50g butter
2 white onions, peeled
2 cloves of garlic, peeled
4 large potatoes, peeled and chopped
700ml chicken or vegetable stock
Bread and butter, to serve

---

1. Preheat your oven to 180°c. Clean and trim the leeks, removing any outer leaves that are unsavoury, as well as the root (but as little as possible, since this is the best bit). Slice into pieces one inch across and toss in oil and salt until evenly coated. Throw into an oven tray and roast for about 20 minutes.

2. Roughly chop the onions and garlic. Melt the butter with a bit of oil in a large saucepan over a medium heat. Add the onion and garlic and cook until golden and tender, about 10 minutes, enough time for the leeks to finish cooking.
3. Add the roasted, slightly charred leeks to the onions and stir to combine. Cook like this for a couple of minutes, then add the potatoes, incorporate them and add enough stock to cover the vegetables plus an inch. Bring to the boil, then reduce the heat and simmer gently for another 20 minutes or until potatoes are tender.
4. Blend about half the vegetables so that the soup still has texture and the liquid is a light green. If you like your soup entirely blended, this is fine.
5. Serve with bread and butter.

Beans à la Gohar

So called because it was the way Laila Gohar taught me, and hundreds of others, during the Covid-19 pandemic, to cook beans. Cooked like this, beans become sweet, salty treats, as exciting as any meat or fish. I have kept the form from my diary of the time. This method of preparing beans works for any of the recipes below.

Soak the desired beans overnight in six times their volume of water. The next morning, or whenever you're ready to cook – they will happily sit for a night and a day – add more water as needed, so the swollen beans have at least a couple of inches of water above them. Add an onion, halved, a carrot, halved, parsley, sage, mint and rosemary tied together, a quarter of a lemon, a generous pinch of salt and an equally generous glug of olive oil. It's not necessary to use lots of fresh herbs – generally, I use only the stalks of soft herbs I've used elsewhere, tied together with string, but a sprig of rosemary or a bay leaf never goes amiss. Really, you can add anything you think will flavour the beans – fennel ends and fronds, fennel seeds too, peppercorns, anything that would be happy in a stock. Boil until the beans are soft – as this differs dramatically not only between types of beans (cannellini, borlotti, et cetera) but between brands of beans too, it is best to begin checking them after twenty minutes. Beans are dynamic – what I add changes every time – and they are forgiving. The liquor from beans is wonderful on its own, eaten with the beans and perhaps some leafy greens, but can also serve as a vegetable stock. Interestingly, chickpeas cooked with lemon, onion, garlic and rosemary make the best substitute for chicken stock I know. Interesting because chick/en/peas.

Best Beans

The essence of this dish is slow frying and time. I would make it for eight during the first Covid lockdown when, somewhat madly, my siblings, my parents and our respective partners spent four months living in close quarters. Beans cooked like this are good enough to bring a fractious group to the table.

1 large white onion, peeled and diced
4 cloves of garlic, peeled and crushed
Small handful of dry rosemary sprigs
3 tbsp olive oil
3 big beef tomatoes, diced
3 generous ladles of white beans prepared à la Gohar (see opposite), plus 3 ladles of their liquor

1. Sauté the onion, garlic and rosemary sprigs in the olive oil in a heavy pan over a low heat so they are just cooking, essentially bathing in the oil. Stir occasionally.
2. After about 10 minutes, when the onion is translucent and the garlic golden, add the tomatoes. Stir and cook for another 10 minutes on the same very low heat until the tomato has almost melted away.
3. Now stir in the beans and their liquor. Increase the heat for 30 seconds or so to warm them through, then reduce again to very low. Leave to simmer for 15 or so minutes.
4. Serve with bread or rice, any subtle carb, with some lemony chard.

English Summer Minestra

Another Covid lockdown recipe. I began to cook this when the vegetable garden my sister and I planted began to show results, after we had spent many hours tending the land and listening to Doja Cat. It is reviving when served not-quite-hot on a summer evening.

A saucepan of beans prepared à la Gohar (see page 180)
A punnet of cherry tomatoes, halved
A generous glug of olive oil
2 cloves of garlic, peeled and crushed
2 courgettes, finely sliced
A generous pinch of chilli flakes
4 handfuls of brown rice
Bread and butter, to serve

1. In a pan, fry the cherry tomatoes in the olive oil until they begin to release their juices and soften.
2. Add the garlic to the tomatoes, mix together, turn up the heat and cook until most of the juices have gone, then add the courgettes and chilli and incorporate.
3. Pour the liquor from the beans and as many beans as you want into the mixture, cover and bring to the boil. Then add the rice and cook, with the lid on, until the rice is soft, adding more water if necessary.
4. Serve with buttered sourdough bread.

Plum Bruised Shin

This is a bastardisation of various stews – one cooked by my grandfather, one of beef cheek, from northern Italy, and a few others besides. The addition of plums is my own. The plums used here are the fat yellowish ones found in Barcelona in the autumn, but any will do. A good butcher will sell you beef fat – the sort they use to wrap roasting joints, not something already melted like dripping. This dish fed thirty hungry Catalans on a hot evening in the garden.

SERVES A CROWD

2.5kg beef shin, cut in thick slices
500g beef fat, cubed
2 tbsp seasoned flour
Olive oil
6 white onions, peeled and roughly chopped
1 head of garlic, cloves peeled and crushed
6 x 400g tins of whole tomatoes, blitzed
20 yellow plums, halved and stoned
⅓ a bottle (about 250ml) of red wine
Bread and butter, to serve

---

1. Toss the shin slices and beef fat in seasoned flour, then fry, in batches in a large saucepan, until browned. Set aside.
2. In the same pan, fry the onions and garlic until golden and translucent, then add the tomatoes and cook down until reduced by half.

3. Preheat the oven to 110°c.
4. Add back the beef and fat, stir, then transfer to a roasting pan along with the plums and the wine, combining everything thoroughly.
5. Put in the oven and roast for a minimum of 5 hours: the longer you cook it, the better the beef will be. Any time it seems a little dry, add more red wine.
6. Serve with vegetables, a little bread and polenta.

Pies and Tarts

HOUSE PASTRIES

Butter Pastry

This pastry is excellent both savoury and sweet, is much stronger than shortcrust, and is so versatile that it's the only white pastry I make. It freezes well and most of the time I have a ball of it in my freezer. When thick it's indulgent, when rolled thin it's crisp. Always wash it with a beaten egg. If you add a tablespoon of sugar to the flour, it makes an excellent dessert crust. If you have one, steps one to three can be done in a stand mixer using a dough hook attachment.

130g butter
330g plain flour
A pinch of salt
1 egg, beaten

---

1. Rub the butter into the flour along with the salt until combined and crumbly.
2. Add the beaten egg and, gradually, up to 40ml of cold water.
3. Knead until the dough comes together, then leave in the fridge for an hour or so to cool.
4. If you want to leave it in the fridge or freezer for much longer, put it into a bag or wrap it.
5. Roll thick or thin and use the offcuts for decoration.

Olive Oil Pastry

This is my other house pastry, which I use for rich savoury tarts. The restraint of the brown flour and the crispness leant by the olive oil are foil for gluttony. If you can't find plain wholemeal flour, sift wholemeal bread flour. This recipe is inspired by one on a blog called Chocolate and Zucchini and is still bookmarked. Thank you, Clothilde.

250g plain wholemeal flour
A pinch of salt
60ml olive oil

1. Combine the ingredients in a large bowl with 120ml cold water and knead until you have a soft, smooth dough.
2. Wrap and put in the fridge for an hour, or until needed.
3. Roll quite thin. Brush with beaten egg for a golden brown finish or with olive oil for an earthy brown.

THE SAVOURY GALETTE

A galette is an excellent way to gesture toward a pie, with less work. Here are two suggestions, but almost anything will go in.

Forest and Meadow

Because wild garlic is fleeting it's overused, but should not be dismissed because of this. If you have no wild garlic, replace it with equal parts of the other greens and add three cloves of minced garlic. The tips of nettles are best, more tender; their sting disappears quickly when met with hot water. Big dandelion leaves are less bitter. Eat this tart in the meadow where you picked the dandelions, beside the forest of nettles and wild garlic.

1 medium onion, peeled and chopped
Olive oil
A big basket of wild garlic, nettles and dandelion greens (the ratio I used is about three-sixths wild garlic, two-sixths nettles and one-sixth dandelion greens; add more dandelions for bitterness)
A generous glug of dry white vermouth
Sea salt and freshly ground black pepper
½ a block of feta (about 100g)
A ball of Olive Oil Pastry (see page 189)
2 eggs, beaten

1. Sweat the onion in a glug of olive oil in a large frying pan until translucent, then add the greens, roughly and distractedly chopped, along with the vermouth.
2. When everything is blanched, taste and season, then crumble in the feta and preheat your oven to 180°c.
3. While the oven heats, roll out your pastry into a sort of square, but really any shape; neatness is not needed here. Transfer it to a baking sheet.
4. Add most of the beaten egg, reserving a little for brushing, to the greens to bind them. Spoon the greens into the middle of the pastry, spreading them out a little but making sure to have a generous mound. Roughly fold the pastry over so that you have some of the greens still showing. Brush with the reserved beaten egg.
5. Bake in the oven until the pastry is golden, about 30 minutes.
6. Serve with new potatoes and mayonnaise.

Leek, Honey and Anchovy Galette

The mix of honey and anchovy has an ancient Roman aspect, a time when salty fish was often accompanied with the almost sickly sweet.

4 leeks, rinsed and sliced
Olive oil
1 tbsp honey
A 28g tin of anchovies in olive oil
Freshly ground black pepper
A generous grating of nutmeg
A ball of Olive Oil Pastry (see page 189)
1 egg, beaten

---

1. Soften the leeks in a pan with a splash of olive oil. When they're about halfway cooked, add the honey, the oil from the anchovy tin, pepper and some nutmeg, and continue to cook until very soft. Let the mixture cool.
2. Preheat the oven to 180°c.
3. Roll the pastry out into a circle about 30cm across, transfer to a baking sheet lined with greaseproof paper and make a mound of the leeks in the middle, then arrange the anchovies over the top in a cross-hatch pattern.
4. Fold the pastry edges over roughly and glaze them with the beaten egg. Bake in the oven for an hour or so, until the pastry is crisp and golden.

Meat

I used to frequent a traditional butcher on Bethnal Green Road, a few doors down from the Ayrubi grocery, a shop that runs with great efficiency and almost no waste. Both stood opposite a rather depressing big Tesco, presenting a popular front. The butcher, a man who looked like a butcher – rotund in a healthy-ish way, red-faced with porcine eyes – would indulge my many questions and chat with me when the store wasn't busy. Ox and cow's cheeks, he told me, used to be thrown away or used for dog food until the 2000s, but now – he thought this was funny – they cost the same as a reputable meat like shin and were in high demand. Pork, on the other hand, had fallen gigantically from grace, its prices changing only a little in the forty-something years he'd had the shop. From Thursdays, the shop would be bustling and he'd be joined by three or four assistants, all cutting and sawing and serving. He seemed to reserve a special warmness for the older ladies, the East Enders, who would come in and buy two thin lamb chops, two thin pork chops, enough mince for a shepherd's pie, steak bavette and so on, and slowly count out change to the penny. I'd often go in at lunch and find him eating eggs and sausages from orange Styrofoam, delivered to him by E. Pellici, for whom he made the sausages. When I returned home after a New Year spent cooking in Italy, I walked down Bethnal Green to buy eggs from him and was happy to see pheasants strung up outside. The shop was bustling but he was absent, and there were no eggs. He had died, I discovered, and there was no one to take over his shop. A place of meeting and community gone and not replaced.

A Fiver a Pheasant

My butcher used to sell a brace of pheasants for five pounds, which made me consider eating pheasant every day – pheasant, cabbage, lentils. However, my interest in frugality and seasonality wanes after a few days and might begin to itch against the wishes of my guests and, most importantly, Lo'. Pheasants are skinned rather than plucked and it's quite an easy business, though the squeamish among you may wish to buy them pre-drawn. There are brilliant instructional videos for drawing pheasants on YouTube, presented by men in wax jackets and corduroys who you'd hate to be stuck next to in a pub.

4 pheasants and their edible organs
½ a bottle (375ml) of dry white vermouth (or more)
1 white onion, halved
4 cloves of garlic, halved
A sprig of oregano
A sprig of sage
Sea salt
Olive oil
300g bacon trimmings, smoked or unsmoked as dictated by preference and availability

---

1. Place the pheasants, skinned and gutted, with their edible organs into a roasting dish along with enough white vermouth to cover them by half, and the onion, garlic, oregano, sage and a large pinch of salt. Leave overnight, refrigerated.

2. Before you want to cook the pheasant, pour off the marinade ingredients, aside from the aromatics, and leave aside – you will use it to make the sauce.
3. Preheat the oven to 200°c.
4. Rub the birds in olive oil, then generously layer with thick pieces of bacon. For something like this I tend to use bacon trimmings or bits. They are often fattier, but more importantly are cheap, and you are sometimes lucky enough to get big bits or cured pork, which you can slice thickly yourself. Ask your butcher, since they're not always on display.
5. Having prepared the birds, roast them at 200°c for around 30 to 45 minutes. Check them yourself, since pheasants are so different in size that the cooking time will vary. The flesh should still have a touch of pink.
6. Leave the cooked birds to rest for 10 or so minutes, then mix the juices from the roasting dish with the reserved vermouth, bring it to the boil and reduce by half to make a sauce.

King Charles I's Folly – or a Roast Chicken

I think I have cooked more roast chicken than any other meat, and each time I am surprised by this wonderful bird. King Charles I was, it's said, discovered by the Roundheads because he ordered roast chicken at an inn, at a time when only aristocrats ate the bird. I cannot help imagining the third Charles making a similar faux-pas. The polenta gives the skin an extra crispiness; the onions inside keep it moist.

A handful of rosemary
½ a bulb of garlic
7 onions, halved and peeled
½ a lemon
A good-sized chicken, preferably corn-fed
A fistful of polenta
Sea salt
Olive oil

---

1. Preheat your oven to 200°c.
2. Place the rosemary, garlic, one onion and the half lemon in the chicken's cavity, then rub it all over with polenta, salt and olive oil.
3. Put the chicken in a roasting dish, lay the rest of the onions beside it, and add a splash of water. Roast for 45 minutes, or until the chicken juices run clear, then let it sit for 10 minutes.
4. Serve with a simple green salad and roasted new potatoes.

Rabbit, Plums and Peaches – a Faux Catalan Dish

We had butter to use up – we'd bought it thinking of making a cake, but hadn't. So I fried the base in butter rather than oil. Not a bad thing. Equally important – I think – is the thick stoneware pot, the sort Patience Gray raves about in Honey from a Weed. *I was doubtful about the importance of such pots for a while, but now I know that there is something about the consistent temperature they achieve, some magic inherent in cooking with clay rather than metal. Perhaps because clay is an organic substance and the food is therefore less far from its dirt.*

A generous knob of butter
A drizzle of olive oil
3 white onions, peeled and quartered
4 tomatoes, roughly chopped
4 cloves of garlic, peeled and roughly chopped
4 cooking chorizo, each sliced into 3 pieces
1 rabbit, including the head and offal, jointed
2 large glasses (about 500ml) of white wine (I used a beautiful, very cheap orange-ish white wine from the Catalan hills; I doubt you will find it anywhere else)
A sprig of rosemary
2 large peaches, quartered
4 plums, halved
A large bunch of green grapes

1. Throw the butter and oil into the pot – or into an ovenproof pan if you don't have a gas hob, since a clay pot won't work on electric or induction – and, when the butter has melted, follow with the onions, tomatoes and garlic. This is not a proper sofrito, but nods towards one.
2. When the onions have a little colour, add the chorizo. Roughly chop the rabbit's liver, heart, et cetera and throw in. When they have coloured, tip all this into another pan.
3. Add a touch more butter and brown the rabbit pieces – you may need to do this in two goes. When done, put the onions et cetera back in the pot, bring to a high heat while knocking everything about for 30 seconds or so, then add the wine, 500ml water and the rosemary.
4. Bring to the boil, then reduce to a simmer. Add the quartered peaches and the halved plums and stir in. Now, gently, place the grapes atop the stew and put in the oven for 2 hours. In Catalonia I had an ancient gas oven that had to be lit with a long lighter through a hatch at its bottom. I think the temperature was about 150°c.
5. Now serve – if not eating family style, it would be good to try and give each person a bit of peach, a bit of rabbit and some sausage, and to serve the grapes on their own plate. This goes well with quick-fried courgettes and roast potatoes and hazelnuts. Make sure to give the least squeamish person the head – it is very good.

Duck Presented in a Classical Manner

We made this for the Easter Sunday of the first Covid lockdown, when we had nothing to think of but our table and stomachs. The duck's luxuriant flesh is supplied with whimsy by the addition of primroses.

A spring duck, the largest you can get
Fennel tops
A sprig of rosemary
A handful of sage leaves
6 rashers of bacon, smoked or unsmoked as dictated by preference and availability, roughly chopped
Sea salt
A glass (about 150ml) of red wine
100 primrose flowers

---

1. Preheat the oven to 200°c.
2. Stuff the duck with the fennel, rosemary, sage, bacon and its own innards, roughly chopped. If you are worried about escaping stuffing, you can close the cavity with toothpicks.
3. Rub the duck all over with salt and place, on a rack with a heatproof dish beneath it, in the oven for 40 minutes, until the duck is browned.
4. Remove from the oven, pour the juices into a jug and mix with the wine. Reduce the oven temperature to 150°c. Baste

the duck with the wine mixture, return it to the oven and cook for another 2 to 2 hours and 30 minutes, basting every 20 minutes or so, until the skin is crispy.
5. The duck will now be terribly tender. When it has cooled enough to touch, press the primroses onto the duck's skin, then repeat, pressing new flowers over the old, which will have become translucent. These will retain their colour.
6. Serve the duck surrounded by more flowers, with potatoes, green vegetables and mayonnaise.

Vegetables

Rather than offering a list of recipes, this section has very few and otherwise covers the simple ways I prepare vegetables to accompany a meal's central dish, whether meat, a tart or butter beans. Each would also be found alongside a starch – polenta, bread, rice or potatoes – to complete the plate's trifecta, its meat and two veg. Suitable vegetables are listed, though not exhaustively, beneath each preparation.

VEGETABLE SALADS

Hard vegetables are best prepared with a very sharp knife, or for ease and speed, a mandoline. Once they are finely sliced, they can be tossed with good oil and salt. Vinegar or lemon juice can be added to soften and sharpen the taste.

Salad Baronne

A small red cabbage, about the size of 2 fists
1 tbsp wholegrain mustard (I use Maille)
1 tsp fine salt
150ml white wine vinegar or cider vinegar

---

1. Quarter the cabbage and use a mandoline to cut it into thin slices.
2. Mix in the rest of the ingredients and leave to rest for half an hour.

You can replace the red cabbage with white cabbage, fennel or grated carrot for a similar effect. Raw vegetables pair nicely with rich meats and stews, especially in summer when one might need some relief, an effect intensified by vinegar or lemon. Capers make an excellent addition to fennel, while raisins complement carrots. Fresh leafy herbs can be added for complexity in summer, and spices in winter.

As well as taste, the addition of enough vinegar will slightly pickle some vegetables – cabbage especially – meaning they can be kept for weeks. This being the case, I always have a stoneware jar of Salad Baronne in my fridge and eat it with everything.

carrot | red and white cabbage | celery | fennel | kohlrabi | celeriac | beetroot

LEAF SALADS

I make two sorts of leaf salad: chopped and whole.

Chopped salad is made by chopping different leaves finely alongside herbs to make a flavourful salad that could be eaten with a spoon. Such a salad benefits from oil, salt and vinegar, but does not need the richness of a vinaigrette. A chopped salad would suit a tart, or anything dry really, but nothing with a sauce.

> dil | mint | rocket | parsley | coriander | kale | mustard greens | gem lettuce

One kind of leafy salad is made with soft leaves that are whole or ripped for management: ripping, rather than chopping, maintains the organic look a leafy salad should have. For this reason, leaves should be stripped, or a head of lettuce taken apart, by hand. Such salads can be made of one attractive leaf or a mix of a few. Leaf salads should be dressed with a sweet, rich vinaigrette, which is not mixed in until you're just about to eat, as it will make the leaves soggy.

> oakleaf lettuce | beetroot leaves | radicchio | rocket | chicory | romaine

For a salad of crisper leaves, especially Italian bitters, follow the same method, but pair with a mayonnaise-based dressing, which can be enriched with anchovies. If you want to serve a salad of radicchio, if it's still in vogue, soak it in water for an hour to remove some of its bitterness.

> radicchio | chicory | escarole | Castelfranco | endive

ISSY'S SALAD

And then there's puntarelle. Strictly speaking, it's the heart of the *cicoria asparago* and it's prepared by stripping away the leafy outer stalks – these should be kept and eaten too – until you get to what look like stems morphing into hollow asparagus. Slice these into ribbons and leave to soak for two hours, then drain, dry and serve with a dressing of olive oil, Dijon mustard, capers, anchovies, lemon juice and fresh mayonnaise, in quantities of your choosing.

BLANCHED

To blanch vegetables, bring a large saucepan of well-salted water, more than enough, to a roiling boil and briefly submerge the vegetables (for thirty seconds to two minutes), before draining them through a colander into a sink.

Those too big to be blanched whole should be cut down to size, while those small enough to cook quickly are kept whole. Most will need a little tidying up – the tough ends of runner beans, the tops of carrots – and those with tough skin should be peeled.

> green cabbage | broccoli | kale | asparagus |
> Brussels sprouts | carrots | spinach | corn

Vegetables blanched in salted water generally need nothing added when they accompany a rich dish or sit beside a sauce. If I'm feeling particularly indulgent I might add a little butter, and if I want to sharpen their taste, some lemon. Any more would render the method's genius – retaining flavour as honestly as possible – superfluous and risk unbalancing your plate.

However, corn on the cob does warrant a great deal of butter and should not be chopped up, but served whole. As does asparagus which, if of a good quality, should be served alone before the main.

FRIED

A method Felix Conran taught me for enhancing blanched asparagus and green beans – fry your vegetables in very hot olive oil in a large frying pan, for thirty seconds to a minute and a half, until they begin to char. Their natural sweetness will be offset, their appearance transformed, and they will benefit greatly from a little olive oil and rock salt.

asparagus | broad beans | mange tout |
purple sprouting broccoli | courgette

Otherwise, mushrooms come to mind. But it would be foolish to cast the noble fungi in an accompanying role: it is too good and too rich and so commands the centre. And yet, there is only one recipe for mushrooms in this book: why? It is simple. Whenever I buy – or, better, am given – good mushrooms, I cannot do anything but fry them in butter, plenty of it, over a medium heat, until they are a little crispy but not dried out. Occasionally, I may add some sage leaves or garlic to the butter, but that is all. Another person might add parsley or tarragon, another still, double cream.

ROASTED

Roasting is good for a busy host, since it continues in the background, needing little attention save an occasional shake of the pan and a glance to check that nothing's burning.

To roast root vegetables, I cut them into just-over-bite-sized pieces and evenly coat them in olive oil and salt. An even coating is best achieved by mixing the vegetables by hand in a bowl and will never be had by drizzling oil over vegetables as they lie on their tray. Before you coat the vegetables, place a large tray in the oven and pour in a little oil. For even cooking, the most important thing is that your tray is not overcrowded: it should contain one level of vegetables only and they shouldn't be touching. Cooking for 45 minutes at 180°c is enough for most. Less if they're smaller, more if larger.

beetroot | parsnip | turnip | swede | carrot | onion | celeriac | Jerusalem artichokes

For crispier skin and a quicker roasting time, parboil them first, as in the next recipe.

British Roast Potatoes

I did not think much of the British style for quite a while, preferring the oilier potatoes I'd had in Italy and Spain, cooked close together from raw. Then a deep pull – from the ground? – brought me back. These are crisp on the outside and fluffy within – they are perfect.

1kg potatoes, peeled and chopped into 4
Sea salt
2 good glugs of olive oil

---

1. Boil the potatoes in salted water until they begin to disintegrate very slightly, about 15 minutes.
2. Meanwhile, pour a good glug of olive oil into a roasting dish and put it in an oven at 180°c.
3. When the potatoes are done, drain them in a colander and return them to the saucepan to mix them, gently, with another glug of oil, then place onto the roasting dish. Do not crowd them!
4. Cook for 30 minutes or until they're crispy, shaking the dish after 5 minutes and then every 10 minutes or so to stop them from sticking.

A roasted root should replace your starch rather than your green vegeable. They take spices like za'atar and ras-el-hanout, and herbs like sage and rosemary, well, though make sure these don't overwhelm the rest of the plate.

Prepare and roast small green vegetables in much the same way as root vegetables, but give them half the time in the oven. They will exhibit a caramel sweetness not apparent with other preparations, and do well accompanying something light like fish. They are good with lemon. Often, some of them will burn to a crisp and need to be discarded.

broccoli | cauliflower | Brussels sprouts | green beans | asparagus | celery

When you roast more than one vegetable together, be aware that they cook at different speeds.

Roast cabbage is also a delicious surprise, made by quartering a cabbage, coating it in oil and salt and roasting for half an hour. It is grand enough to be a dinner's centre, but has no fat or protein and must therefore remain auxiliary. The same method and the same sentiment can be applied to squashes, whose flesh becomes soft and sweet, while roast onions turn almost to jam but have no pretensions of grandeur.

Finally, if I have a lot of different vegetables I'd like to cook – odds and ends or an allotment's harvest – I will crowd them together in a roasting dish, letting them touch and lie atop one another, with plenty of oil and salt. Roasting like this for an hour gives you tender, sweet, soft vegetables. Such medleys take excellently to all manner of herbs and spices and can be elevated with the addition of nuts, crushed and quickly roasted in a pan.

FRUIT SALADS

I hated tomatoes when I was little, but loved the salty, oily juice beneath a tomato salad. I would ask my father why it was so delicious, but there was never a satisfying answer. His tomato salads were then made with sliced tomato, olive oil, salt and a pinch of dried basil, and have changed only with the omission of the dried basil, replaced, when it's in the house, with fresh basil. I wonder now when this omission occurred and imagine it was when the dried herb ran out.

The universal tomato salad is so simple because such great – and deserved – regard is given to the tomato. What I've never understood, however, is why more fresh fruit is not treated thus. In winter, when most things must be cooked, fruit salads become an integral part of my table, providing a much-missed freshness. Apples are sliced thin and served with celery and a vinaigrette; pears with sour cheese and lemon; and oranges with olive oil and salt. Apple and pear take nuts and dried fruit well, while oranges stand staunchly alone, welcoming only a pinch of chilli.

oranges | apples | pears | figs

Sauces

'Pestos'

The most popular pesto comes from Genoa and, in its modern incarnation, should be made from basil, pine nuts, Parmesan, pecorino sardo and olive oil. My father would make such a pesto when I was little, with two basil plants from the supermarket, in a white pestle and mortar that was otherwise used to store garlic. When I moved to London I found that pine nuts were off-puttingly expensive and that basil, in quantities I wanted, cost a great deal more than the lavish bunches of hardier herbs from the Turkish supermarket.

And so I began to experiment: I used walnuts, Brazil nuts and cashews alongside mint, dill and coriander. I didn't have a pestle and mortar, so I used my blender, creating a fine pesto. If I lacked Parmesan, I'd replace its sweetness with honey or a spoonful of sugar. I found olive oil too bitter, so I would mix it with sunflower oil and a little water. I kept calling these mixtures 'pesto', and defended this with a general interpretation of the word, which means 'to pound, to crush'. I would also point out that substitution is nothing new: the first recorded recipe for pesto alla Genovese allows for oregano or parsley if basil is not to hand. So what if I took this to the extreme? My pestos taste good on pasta, novel and fresh, and so it hardly matters that their lineage could only be traced through my memory.

A bunch of mint
A bunch of dill
A generous glug of olive oil
A generous glug of sunflower oil
A handful of walnuts
1 tsp salt

1 tbsp honey
⅓ of a clove of garlic
Juice of ½ a lemon

---

1. Strip the mint from its stalks and add to your blender, followed by the dill, roughly chopped up.
2. Add the olive oil, sunflower oil, walnuts, salt, honey, garlic and lemon juice.
3. Blend. Taste the mixture and add more of the ingredients to taste.

The herbs can be replaced with any other, even a little fresh rosemary or sage, though using basil would be something of a waste. Basil's subtle flavour is, after all, best suited to pesto alla Genovese.

My pestos are a key component of my repertoire. They can be used on pasta or gnocchi, but are just as suited to beans and vegetables, roasted and blanched, stirred through rice or adorning new potatoes. For more punch, to accompany meat or fish, add capers, mustard and more lemon. If I want a rougher texture, I'll chop some of the herbs and nuts with a knife. If I wasn't so lazy a cook, I'd chop them all.

Mayonnaise

The first time I made a good mayonnaise was in Ireland. I was nervous, since my previous attempts had ended in failure – liquid mixes of egg and oil, useless and wasteful. But as the rain fell outside, the emulsion came together, a miracle. I'm pretty sure I was using a recipe by Delia Smith that included powdered mustard, though needing a recipe seems strange, the method now so deep in muscle memory.

Eggs are the most important ingredient. They seem a touch resistant to emulsification for a couple of days after they're laid. Old or poor-quality eggs make a mayonnaise that's insipid in taste and colour. The oil you use depends on preference: I tend toward half olive oil and half sunflower oil, since I find a mayonnaise made solely with olive oil too heavy. It is gratifying to know that oils other than olive were historically used in northern France, just as cider was more common than wine. The addition of mustard is only necessary for a mayonnaise made with a very light oil, while the pasted garlic is non-negotiable. It's pleasing to make mayonnaise with a hand whisk, but hard work, so I use the electric whisk attachment of my stand mixer. An egg beater works just as well, as does a blender.

The more yolks, the more certain the emulsion. So I'd start with the quantities below.

4 egg yolks
½ a clove of garlic
A generous pinch of fine salt
Dijon mustard (optional)
About 100ml olive oil

About 100ml sunflower oil
¼ of a lemon (at minimum)

---

1. Put your yolks in a bowl with high sides.
2. Paste your garlic by smashing it on a board, chopping it vigorously, sprinkling it with salt and running your knife over it, backwards and forwards, ten times. Add it to the bowl, along with a pinch of salt and, if using, the mustard.
3. Mix together with your whisk and begin to pour in the oil in the slowest trickle you can manage. A stand mixer is helpful here as you can concentrate completely on this somewhat tricky manoeuvre.
4. If your emulsion fails, remove the oily mixture from the bowl and add a new yolk, then start whisking and pour the oily mixture back in very slowly as you would the oil. A failed emulsion generally comes from adding the oil too quickly, but it can also come from using too large a bowl. If you keep struggling, a spoonful of Dijon mustard will often help.
5. When the emulsion catches, the mixture should turn firm and creamy and you can begin to pour a little more quickly and alternate the oils. But be cautious – too much oil, too quickly, will reverse the emulsion.
6. Once you've added all the oil you should have a thick mayonnaise and can adjust it for salt.

Add more oil for a lighter mayonnaise and more lemon for a tarter one. A good dressing can be made by reintroducing some of the egg white and slowly mixing it in. For a mayonnaise to accompany fish, add chopped parsley, and for chicken, tarragon. Capers will enhance both. For potatoes, add chopped mint and dill; and for beef, horseradish. More garlic can be added to taste, as long as it's pasted, though it will never result in an aioli, which is made without eggs. The addition of more lemon juice, Heinz ketchup and a little paprika makes Marie Rose sauce an undeniably good accompaniment to prawns.

Mayonnaise can accompany almost anything and in summer, when casseroles and stews lose their appeal, it is never far from my dinner table. It is especially necessary alongside tarts and pies, since they have no juice to meld them with the other food.

Desserts

Desserts often make cooks anxious because they lean toward chemistry – they can't be adjusted or tried while they cook. Cooking the same desserts over and over, ones you know by rote, frees you from this fear and allows the sort of personalisation and ingenuity, generally reserved for expert cooks.

House Cake

My house cake is made from a simple base to which many alterations and additions can be made. Elegantly, it's made of equal amounts butter, sugar and flour, though I only realised this after making it for two years. And more recently still, my brother told me this makes it a pound cake, which I'd imagined to be something else completely. I can't remember where the original recipe came from, which tends to mean I found it somewhere online. One day, I'd like to write letters of thanks to every food blogger whose recipe has become part of my repertoire, for they have provided me with as much as any culinary grandmother could. The first time I wrote down the recipe it was like this:

2 apples, peeled and cored
2 pears, peeled and cored
120g unsalted butter
2 eggs
120g caster sugar
Trifle sherry, to taste
120g self-raising flour
½ tsp baking powder
A pinch of salt

---

1. Preheat the oven to 180°c. Line the bottom of a 20 centimetre round cake tin with greaseproof paper.
2. Chop your apples and pears into rough 'squares', avoiding uniformity, and set aside.

3. Melt the butter in a pan and, when liquid, take off the heat.
4. In a large bowl, whisk the eggs with the sugar and a generous glug of trifle sherry.
5. When frothy, add about half of the flour, the baking powder and roughly half the melted butter, continuing to whisk. When combined, add the rest of the flour and butter along with a pinch of salt and combine fully. Using a spoon, mix the apples and pears in, making sure they are evenly distributed.
6. Pour the batter into the lined tin and bake in the preheated oven for just under an hour, foiling the top if it begins to burn. When it's ready, a skewer inserted into the middle ought to come out clean.

The possibilities of this cake are immense. You can swap the fruit for another – I often add frozen blueberries, because we usually have them in the freezer, but any other frozen berry will do, and their size means they needn't be defrosted. Plums and peaches work too, and can all be poached first to enhance their flavour. However, it would not suit citrus fruit.

The butter can be infused – with herbs and more excitingly by using it to poach the fruit you'll add to the cake, though if you do this, you'll need to add 50g more butter. This gives the crumb the fruit's flavour while making the fruit especially rich.

The cake can be flavoured with spices – za'atar is particularly good – and other alcohols – Campari works well, while Cinzano (a bitter liquor made from artichokes) is too intense. Equally, the alcohol can be omitted completely. If you don't have self-raising flour, add another teaspoon of baking powder; ditto if you want to use half wholemeal flour. The cake is excellent alone, served with cream, yoghurt and, especially, custard.

Thick Custard

For a long time I was worried about making my own custard, believing it to be hard. It is not! All it requires is time and a little attention to detail, but since the cooking is gentle, there is not much that can go wrong. For a plain custard, skip the infusion but still warm your cream before you add it to the eggs and sugar. It is worth using very good eggs because you will get a wonderful golden colour – the dimmer the eggs, the dimmer the custard.

There is nothing better than a proper custard, nothing that speaks more of the oft-missed genius of the British kitchen.

600ml double cream
A handful of rosemary
2 whole eggs
2 egg yolks
150g caster sugar

---

1. Infuse the cream with the rosemary for an hour by leaving it in a homemade bain-marie – made by setting a deep heatproof bowl over a pan of simmering water, ensuring that the bottom of the bowl is not touching the water beneath – and stirring it every now and then.
2. Beat together the whole eggs, egg yolks and sugar in a metal or glass bowl and place this above a saucepan of simmering water, making sure the water does not touch the bowl.
3. Slowly add the cream, beating it in now and then, until it is all

mixed together. Leave for an hour or so until thickened, giving it a beating every 20 minutes – it will begin sticking to the bottom. This is fine.

I tend to make my custard ahead of time, either putting it on before I begin cooking everything else, or doing it the day before and refrigerating it. Reheat it in a bain-marie, or serve cold or at room temperature. Excellent with poached pears, a reasonably plain cake or by itself. The rosemary can be swapped for a floral or another herb, though I don't recommend basil.

Flavoured Whipped Cream

This is a method I came up with after Lo' discovered that cream can't be whipped after it's been heated up. She had been trying to infuse the cream for my birthday cake, which sat – gigantic and naked – in the main room, much admired by the unknowing guests who had begun arriving with murderous regularity.

---

1. Make a strong syrup by mixing one part sugar and one part water and whatever you want to infuse it with – sage, cherries, orange peel, et cetera – in a saucepan, bringing it to the boil and leaving it to simmer for an hour or more. You'll want roughly 100ml of syrup for every litre of cream you plan to whip. Let the water reduce by two-thirds but don't let the pan dry out, since the sugar will burn and be almost impossible to remove. Leave to cool, completely.
2. Once the syrup is cool, prepare to whip the cream. Have a small glass of syrup, about 100ml, beside you when you start and when the cream begins to come together add a little of the syrup and whip some more. Continue until the syrup has gone and your cream has attained stiff peaks. If the syrup has colour, the cream will take it on, almost invisibly. It will be suffused by a light, almost vacant, flavour.

Whipping cream is a delicate business and requires constant attention, for it changes from fluffy to curdled in an instant. Although lightly curdled whipped cream is fine to eat and can still top a cake, it takes on an undesirable texture and lacks sheen.

POACHED FRUIT

My poaching liquid sits in an unmarked jar in my fridge, the culmination of the months of fruit poaching since I ruined its predecessor. With this liquid I begin each fresh poaching, topping it up with more orange peel, alcohol (generally whatever scraps of wine or fragrant spirits are knocking around), spices (cloves, star anise, cinnamon), sugar and water.

Into a saucepan of this liquid, place a poaching fruit, listed below, bring to the boil and then reduce to a simmer. Poached fruit generally need about an hour, but can be left for much longer on a low heat. Unripe fruit poaches well, though it may need a little more time, while overripe fruit will fall to pieces. Pears should be peeled with their stalk left on, and stone fruit should be stoned and, when large enough, halved. Interesting colour effects can be had on the white skin of a pear: a red liquid will turn the flesh a gentle pink, while saffron dyes it gold.

pears | peaches | nectarines | plums | cherries | rhubarb | figs | apricots | strawberries

Poached fruit is an excellent dessert if you're strapped for cash or time: it is easy, cheap and very dignified. Traditional poaching spices speak of mediaeval cookery, but can be replaced. Poached fruit is best served atop custard on a little plate, where it sits as a flash of colour on a placid background.

Trifle

Trifle is the sum of its parts made heroic by their association – the great triumph of British desserts, without complexity, without conceit; in a word, simple. And since it is simple, each part must be excellent.

My trifle is indebted to Fergus Henderson and Trevor Gulliver's excellent recipe. Actually, a great deal of what I think about my country's food is part of a conversation that began when they opened their restaurant in 1994, the year of my birth.

The trifle sponge, an eggy and slightly heavy cake, perfectly calibrated to take on sherry, is taken from The Book of St John, *with alterations to reflect my own style.*

Trifle sponge
5 free-range eggs
160g caster sugar
35g butter, melted
160g plain flour
A pinch of salt

Trifle nuts
A handful of nuts, roughly chopped or flaked
A splash of sherry
Sea salt

To assemble
More sherry
Poached fruit (see page 227)

Thick custard, infused as you choose (see page 224)
Flavoured whipped cream (see page 226)

---

1. Line a 20 centimetre square cake tin with baking parchment and preheat your oven to 180°c.
2. Beat the eggs and sugar over the heat in a homemade bain-marie (see page 224) until they have doubled in size. You will certainly need an electric whisk for this process.
3. Fold the melted butter, flour and salt into the mixture with a metal spoon and gentle care, until just incorporated. Pour into the lined tin and bake in the oven for 30 to 35 minutes, until a skewer inserted into the middle of the sponge comes out clean, then allow to cool.
4. Toss a handful of nuts into a frying pan, add a splash of sherry and a pinch of salt, and cook over a low heat until lightly browned. They'll be sweet and a little salty, with an aftertaste of alcohol.
5. To assemble, find a large bowl – a glass one is pretty, but not even I have one that's right, so don't worry – and break up the trifle sponge in its bottom, to achieve an even-ish coverage. Pour over a generous amount of sherry, but not so much that the sponge becomes soggy. On top of the sponge lay your poached fruit, on top of the fruit your infused custard, and on top of the custard your flavoured cream. Make sure to use compassionate flavours in the cream and custard – a herb and a flower – or omit the flavouring from one. Sprinkle with trifle nuts and put to bed in the fridge, to be served the next day.

Sticky Toffee Pudding

A Brazilian artist came to dinner one night, and when I asked her what she'd like to eat she said sticky toffee pudding, which was 'like a poem, with a name from Joyce'. I had never made it before, so I adapted the recipe from Jane Grigson's English Food, *which she took from the pudding's inventor. She says it was exciting after the privations of the Second World War, but to me it's a recipe that makes things go far – full of water and with a sauce, which economises on butter and cream. It is odd: rather than a cake batter you have a sort of soup, and when I first made it I kept thinking I'd made some awful mistake. But fear not, it will set.*

175g pitted dates, stoned and chopped
300ml boiling water
1 tsp bicarbonate of soda
60g butter at room temperature, plus extra for greasing
175g caster sugar
2 eggs, beaten
175g self-raising flour

Sauce
200g soft brown sugar
6 tbsp double cream
140g butter

1. Grease a loose-bottomed 20 centimetre square cake tin with butter. Preheat the oven to 180°c.
2. Put the dates into a pan, pour on the boiling water and bring to the boil again. Remove from the heat, stir in the bicarbonate of soda and leave to stand for 10 minutes.
3. Cream the butter and sugar together, then add the eggs bit by bit. Fold in the flour, then the dates and their juice. Pour into the tin and bake for 30 to 40 minutes, or until a skewer inserted into the middle of the sponge comes out clean.
4. Meanwhile, make the sauce by mixing all the ingredients in a pan and bringing them to the boil, then simmer for 3 minutes. Pour some of the sauce over the cooked pudding, then put it back into the oven for 10 minutes so that the sauce can be absorbed and bubble to a nice golden brown.
5. Serve cut into squares, with the rest of the sauce in a jug.

There's a chaos of departed guests upon the table – dessert plates smeared with custard, pear cores, a Catalan knife precarious beside the edge. The tablecloth, not quite white to begin with, has taken on an expressive nature – deep brown from jus, red from wine. Glasses are empty, save a couple which are too-full, poured by N– who'd had enough but hadn't realised, and most are smeared with lipstick. In the centre, the salt cellar has been knocked asunder and the flakes of Maldon are a snowdrift against the stoneware jug of wild flowers, proud in their wild calm. Another of grandma's coffee cups has broken, but that's OK. Oh, how tired I suddenly am, listening to Lo' brushing her teeth, a plate in my hand. I'd hoped to clear up, but that was another man's hope, and I replace the dirty plate beside an empty packet of cigarettes. That was nice, those were nice people, we have nice friends. I turn off the speaker, remove my trousers and fold them upon a chair, turn off the light, leaving the kitchen window open in hope of a fresh-scented morning.

Index

à la Russe 133–4
ability 111
amaro 13, 152
anchovy, leek and honey galette 192
aperitifs 129
apologies 77
appetite 143, 150
apples 46–7, 150–1, 211, 220–2
apricots 46, 151, 227
aristocracy 104, 133
arrivals 120, 121
artichokes 138, 143
artisan produce 164–6
asparagus 127, 145, 206–7
aubergine 20–2, 108, 170–1

bacon
   all seasons tart 20–2
   classic duck 200–1
   a fiver a pheasant 195–6
basil 211, 214–15
beans 146, 168, 207
   beans à la Gohar 180, 181–3
   best beans 181
   English summer minestra 182–3
beef 35, 70, 75, 93, 138, 146
   borscht 125
   Lowena's birthday sauce 42–3
   plum bruised shin 184–5
   see also steak
beef marrow, pie 33–4
beer 3, 12–13, 23–4, 106, 120, 125, 127, 130

Billingsgate Fish Market 37–8
birthdays 37–43, 142
blanching 206–7
blinis 125
bone marrow 33–4, 115
borscht 125
Bosch 27–8
bread 3, 10, 12, 45, 60, 65, 70, 102, 106, 111, 123, 144
British Army x–xi
budget-constraints 70, 75–6, 105–8, 143, 150–1, 163–4, 195
Bullshit (game) 156
butchers 11–12, 14, 27, 35, 42, 139, 161, 184, 193–4
butter 18, 75, 163, 206–7, 220–2, 230–1
   butter pastry 33–4, 188

cabbage 24
   blanched 4, 146
   buttered 45
   pappardelle alla Danielle 135–6
   roast 210
   see also red cabbage
cacio e pepe 106
cakes 3, 11–12, 57, 61, 75, 109, 141, 148
   birthday 39, 40, 226
   house cake 220–2
cancellations 77, 122
candles 90, 106
card games 154, 155–6
carrots 6–9, 15–18, 52–5, 172–3

beans à la Gohar 180
buttered 146
a cheap but impressive-looking pie 33–4
snacks 143
Categories (game) 155
caviar 39, 76, 125
cavolo nero and farro soup 6–7
celery 6–9, 15–17, 43, 52–3, 172–3, 211
chairs 81–2, 98
Champagne 69, 84, 102, 127
chard 15, 20, 28, 146, 181
Cheddar, all seasons tart 20–2
cheese 10, 44, 45, 60, 75, 76, 93, 102, 106
   bread and 144
   cheese courses 150
   local 125
   see also Cheddar; feta; Parmesan
chicken 18, 45, 93, 102–3, 107, 146
   chicken and rice for when you're sick as a dog 54–5
   King Charles I's folly (a roast chicken) 197
   (not) my mother's chicken soup 52–3
children 62–3
chinaware 84–5
chocolate 75, 84, 105, 148, 151
chorizo, rabbit, plums and peaches 198–9
Christmas 109, 148
cider 29, 146, 216
cleaning up 158–9, 233
cocktails 3, 12–13, 18–19, 29–30, 120
   see also specific cocktails
coffee 4, 13, 18–19, 24, 40, 50, 123, 151–3
Conran, Felix 207
conversation 59, 62, 90, 126
cooperation 115–16
coriander 53–5, 115, 165, 205, 214
corn on the cob 207
courgettes 20–2, 108, 161, 182–3
crabs 38–9, 40
crackers 150
cream 18, 20–2, 75, 224–5, 230–1
   flavoured whipped 226, 229
crisps 3, 12, 23, 24, 48, 73, 123, 143
crumble 24, 148
Cuckoo Wines, Dalston 128–9
cure-all, a 50
curry, green banana 107

custard 24, 109, 148, 224–5, 227, 229
cutlery 84–5, 94, 99

dandelion greens 190–1
dates, sticky toffee pudding 230–1
desserts 4, 24, 30, 106, 148–9, 219–31
dietary requirements 112
digestifs 13, 18–19, 40
dill 11, 25, 52–3, 57, 165–6, 214–15, 218
dinners 1–55, 119–59
   birthdays 37–43
   Friday and Saturday 10–17
   going out after 29–30
   for lovers 44–7
   for the sick and sad 48–55
   Sunday evening 13, 18–22
   weeknight 1, 2–9
dishwashers 158
drinks 127–31
   after-dinner 152
   non-alcoholic 50, 70, 129–30
   stopping serving 157
   and toasting 139–40
   see also beer; spirits; wine
drunkenness 13, 29, 90, 103, 127, 129–30, 153–4, 157–8
duck 12
   classic 200–1

eggs 33–4, 44, 106, 127, 161, 163, 193–4
   all seasons tart 20–2
   custard 224–5
   forest and meadow galette 190–1
   house cake 220–2
   leek, honey and anchovy galette 192
   mayonnaise 216–18
   sticky toffee pudding 230–1
   trifle 228–9
espresso martinis 30
'ethical' shopping 165
eye contact 139–40

families 62
family-style service 134, 137–8
farro and cavolo nero soup 6–7
fennel 43
   all seasons tart 20–2
   beans à la Gohar 180

duck 200–1
feather and stalk soup 176–7
slow-roasted salmon 26
feta 11, 20–2, 190–1
Find the glass (game) 155
fish 12, 31, 37–8, 44, 128, 138
  leek, honey and anchovy galette 192
  slow-roasted salmon 25–6
  tinned 10, 12, 60, 70
flowers 11, 31, 51, 70, 91
  edible 200–1
food shopping 105–6
formal hosting 87, 134
fruit 148, 161, 165
  fruit bowls 4, 151
  fruit salads 211
  poached 3, 227, 228–9
  starters 145
  see also specific fruit

galettes 190–2
  forest and meadow 190–1
  leek, honey and anchovy 192
games 57–8, 153–6
garlic 167
garnishes 168
generosity 70
gifts 68–71, 74
gin 131
glasses 85, 96–7, 99, 120, 131, 139–40
gnocchi 49, 113–14
grapes 51, 150, 198–9
gravy 24, 137, 146
green beans 207
guesting 67–77
guests 57–65, 120–6
  arrivals 120, 121
  getting them to leave 40, 157
  numbers 59–60
  overwhelming 126
  unexpected 65
  what to bring 68–71, 74
  who don't bring anything 129
  who help out 72, 73
  who to invite 61–3
Gulliver, Trevor 228
Gurdjieff 139

ham 45, 106
Hazan, Marcella 113–14
Henderson, Fergus 228
herbs 70, 143, 148
honey 70
  a cure-all 50
  lamb shoulder with honey and wine 46–7
  leek, honey and anchovy galette 192
hoppers 106–7
hosts xi, 1, 104, 157
  anxious/nervous 31, 72, 126
  and budget issues 75–6
  cooperative 115–16
  inexperienced 73
housemates 62

ice 13, 131
ice cream 48, 125
impression-making 31–6
informal hosting 3, 87
ingredients 163–8
  quality of 163–4
'inside picnics' 81–2
introductions 62, 120
invitations 64, 122
Italian food 14, 106, 113, 115, 143, 172–3

jazz 92
juices 50, 70

kitchens 109–10
knives 86–7, 94, 98, 110, 203

lamb 12, 57, 146, 193
  lamb shoulder with honey and wine 46–7
  roast's ragu 8–9
lasagne 24, 49
lateness 77, 121
leaving 40, 157
leeks 146
  leek, honey and anchovy galette 192
  roast leek and potato soup 178–9
lemons 10, 26, 50, 207
lighting 90
local produce 125, 146, 150, 164
London night life 30
lovers, dinners for 44–7

low-carbon produce 164–6
lunches, Sunday 23–8

mains, notes on 146–7
mandolines 203
manners 69, 71–2
margaritas 29
Marie Rose sauce 218
marinades 14–15
markets 37–8, 94, 165–6
martinis 30, 45, 115, 120, 130
  recipe 131
mayonnaise 44, 111, 137, 216–18
measurements 166
meat 106, 128, 137
  cured 144, 161
  local 125
  recipes 193–201
  roast 24, 137
  serving up 137
  see also beef; chicken; lamb; veal
method, notes on 163–8
mint 11, 44, 57, 68, 143, 180, 205, 214–15, 218
mushrooms 33–4, 207
music 73, 74, 92, 119

nettles 190–1
nuts 14–15, 45, 68, 143, 211, 214–15, 228–9

off-licences 128, 129
oils 163, 167, 216–18
olive oil pastry 189
  all seasons tart 20–2
  forest and meadow galette 190–1
  leek, honey and anchovy galette 192
olives 31, 123, 126, 131, 143, 163
oranges 151, 211
organic produce 164–6
orgasm 140
Ottolenghi, Yotam 147
ovens 109–10
ox cheek 193
  ox and pig cheek stew 14–15
oysters 10, 38, 143

parboiling 208
Parmesan 17, 106, 127, 135–6, 214

parsley 53, 165–6, 168, 180, 205, 207, 214, 217
partridge 27
pasta 3, 48, 49, 57, 76, 105–6, 109, 126, 128, 137, 146
  Lowena's birthday sauce 42–3
  pappardelle alla Danielle 135–6
  sauces 42–3, 169–73
  sausage ragu 172–3
  sujuk ragu with wholemeal 'pappardelle' 16–17
  see also lasagne
pastry 188–9
  butter pastry 33–4, 188
  olive oil 20–2, 189–92
pâté 145
peaches 11, 12, 145, 151
  rabbit, plums and peaches 198–9
pears 50, 106, 150–1, 211
  house cake 220–2
  poached 3, 227
peas 4, 45, 137
pesto 57, 105–6, 214–15
pheasant 27, 193–4
  a fiver a pheasant 195–6
pickles 44, 65
pies 187–92
  a cheap but impressive-looking pie 33–4
pigeons 27
pigs
  pig and ox cheek stew 14–15
  suckling 35–6
  see also pork
pine nuts 214
pineapple 151
pizza 105–6
plates 95, 98, 99
plating up 133–4
plums 146
  plum bruised shin 184–5
  rabbit, plums and peaches 198–9
poached fruit 3, 227, 228–9
polenta 4, 27, 138, 146, 197
Poor pussy (game) 155
pork 14–15, 125, 193
  pork belly 84
  suckling pig 35–6
pork sausages 6–7, 16–17, 172–3

240

potatoes 12, 23–4, 44, 75, 102, 107, 137, 146, 161
   feather and stalk soup 176–7
   potato dauphinoise 18, 45, 75
   roast leek and potato soup 178–9
   roast potatoes 146, 209
prawns 38, 105
preferences 104, 112
prep time 4, 11, 18
President (game) 155–6
prosecco 123, 128
prunes 14–15, 47
punctuality 77, 121
puntarelle 206

quail 27–8, 101

rabbit, plums and peaches (a faux Catalan dish) 198–9
radicchio 61, 205
ragu
   roast's ragu 8–9
   sausage ragu 172–3
   sujuk ragu with 'pappardelle' 16–17
ratatouille, a sort of 108
recipes 6–9, 14–17, 20–2, 25–8, 33–6, 42–3, 46–7, 50, 52–5, 108, 135–6, 161–231
red cabbage 102–3, 204
red wine 13, 48, 120, 128
   cavolo nero and farro soup 6–7
   duck 200–1
   Lowena's birthday sauce 43
   plum bruised shin 184–5
   roast's ragu 8–9
   slutty spaghetti 170–1
research 113–14
restaurants 111
reverie 113–14
rice 51, 81
   chicken and rice 54–5
   English summer minestra 182–3
room, the 12, 79–99

sadness, dinners for 48–55
sage 26–7, 46–7, 50, 141, 195–6, 200–1, 207, 209
salads 3, 10, 18, 45, 84, 103
   chopped salads 205

fruit salads 211
Issy's salad 206
leaf salads 205
salad Baronne 35, 204
vegetable salads 203–4
salmon, slow-roasted 25–6
salt 143, 163
sardines 31, 44
saucepans, serving food in 93, 137
sauces 137, 213–18
   Lowena's birthday 42–3
   Marie Rose 218
   pasta 42–3, 169–73
   tomato 106, 113–14
sausages 145, 161, 167, 193
   cavolo nero and farro soup 6–7
   sausage ragu 172–3
   sujuk ragu 16–17
seasonality 164
seating 81–2, 98
second-hand goods 85, 94–7, 99
serving up 132, 137–8
serving ware 93, 137
sex 140
sherry 220–2, 228–9
shoes, removal 71
shyness 31, 72, 126
sick, the, dinners for 48–55
silver 94
simplicity, rule of 18, 31, 45, 102–4, 111, 112, 127, 146–7, 149
Smith, Delia 108, 216
snacks 3, 12, 23–4, 121, 143–5
soup 3, 12, 48, 49, 50, 51, 137, 175–85
   cavolo nero and farro 6–7
   feather and stalk 176–7
   (not) my mother's chicken 52–3
   roast leek and potato 178–9
spaghetti 106, 115
   slutty 170–1
speeches 141–2
spinach 53
spirits 13, 29, 130–1
   see also vodka; whiskey
Spitalfields Market 94
sponge, trifle 228–9
spoons 94
squash 20–2, 210

starters 145
steak 45, 49
stew 3–4, 49, 84, 138–9, 146, 175–85
  ox and pig cheek 14–15
sticky toffee pudding 148, 230–1
stock 168
strawberries 10–12, 75, 148
sujuk ragu with 'pappardelle' 16–17
Sunday evening dinners 13, 18–22
Sunday lunches 23–8
syrup 226

table, the 79–99, 98
  laying 31, 40, 72, 86–7
  makeshift 80–2
tablecloths 81–2, 88, 99
  stains 88
tarts 187–92
  all seasons 20–2
tea 4, 123, 146, 152
tequila 29
theatre 84–5, 93, 103
timings
  desserts 149
  time constraints 105–6, 111
  when to eat 3, 12, 19, 51, 132
toasting 139–40, 142
toilets 92
tomatoes 11, 106
  best beans 181
  cavolo nero and farro soup 6–7
  chicken and rice 54–5
  English summer minestra 182–3
  Lowena's birthday sauce 43
  ox and pig cheek stew 14–15
  plum bruised shin 184–5
  rabbit, plums and peaches 198–9
  roast's ragu 8–9
  sausage ragu 172–3
  slutty spaghetti 170–1
  a sort of ratatouille 108
  sujuk ragu with 'pappardelle' 16–17
  tinned tomatoes 166
  tomato salads 161, 211
  tomato sauce 106, 113–14
travelling 123–5
trifle 148, 228–9
truffle sauce (ready-made) 135–6

veal 35, 106
vegetables 161, 165–6, 203–11
  blanched 4, 146, 206–7
  fried 207
  roasted 208–10
  snacks 143
  starters 145
  vegetable salads 203–4
  see also specific vegetables
vermicelli noodles 53
vermouth 131, 172–3, 190–1, 195–6
vodka 29, 75, 115, 131

walnuts 14–15, 214–15
water 123, 128, 130
wealth 70
weeknight dinners 1, 2–9
what to make 101–16
whiskey 50, 75, 152
white wine 10, 12, 24, 120, 127–8, 153
  chicken and rice 54–5
  chicken soup 52–3
  Friday and Saturday dinners 13
  lamb shoulder with honey and wine 46–7
  pappardelle alla Danielle 135–6
  rabbit, plums and peaches 198–9
  sujuk ragu 16–17
wild garlic 190–1
wine 13, 23, 29, 45, 49, 84, 103, 125, 127–8, 161, 163
  budgeting for 68–9, 75–6, 106, 128–9, 167
  cheap 128–9, 167
  choosing 128–9
  guests' contributions 3, 68–70, 71
  to impress 31
  knowledge of 130
  local 125
  magnums 40, 75
  matching 128
  natural 129
  oxygenation 130
  putting the cork back in 130
  spritzes 3
  stopping serving 157
  for weeknights 2, 3
  see also Champagne; prosecco; red wine; white wine
work 3, 10–11